GREAT LIVES OBSERVED

Gerald Emanuel Stearn, *General Editor*

EACH VOLUME IN THE SERIES VIEWS THE CHARACTER AND ACHIEVE-
MENT OF A GREAT WORLD FIGURE IN THREE PERSPECTIVES—
THROUGH HIS OWN WORDS, THROUGH THE OPINIONS OF HIS CON-
TEMPORARIES, AND THROUGH RETROSPECTIVE JUDGMENTS—THUS
COMBINING THE INTIMACY OF AUTOBIOGRAPHY, THE IMMEDIACY
OF EYEWITNESS OBSERVATION, AND THE OBJECTIVITY OF MODERN
SCHOLARSHIP.

DENIS MACK SMITH, *editor of this volume in the Great Lives
Observed series, is Fellow of All Souls College, Oxford University. Regarded in Italy as the leading authority on Garibaldi and the Italian Revolution, he has published widely in
both English and Italian. His book* Italy, A Modern History
has seen nine editions in Italy alone, and his Garibaldi: A
Great Life in Brief *(Knopf) was greeted by one reviewer as "a
minor masterpiece."*

Forthcoming volumes in the Great Lives Observed series

Booker T. Washington, *edited by Emma Lou Thornbrough*

Huey Long, *edited by Hugh Davis Graham*

John F. Kennedy, *edited by Barton J. Bernstein*

Joseph McCarthy, *edited by Allen Matusow*

Mao, *edited by Jerome Ch'en*

Woodrow Wilson, *edited by John Braeman*

ITALY AND HER NEIGHBORS (1850)

GREAT LIVES OBSERVED

GARIBALDI

Edited by DENIS MACK SMITH

A SPECTRUM BOOK

PRENTICE-HALL, INC., ENGLEWOOD CLIFFS, N.J.

Most of the documents included in this volume have been translated from the original French, Italian, and German by the editor. Where documents are already translated, their source is given. Where the original is in English, a very few minor changes of spelling and punctuation have been introduced for the sake of consistency. Explanations inserted in the text by the editor are enclosed in brackets.

Current printing (last number):
10 9 8 7 6 5 4 3 2

Library of Congress Catalog Card Number: 69-15335

2-28-74

Printed in the United States of America

Prentice-Hall International, Inc., London

Contents

v

7

Garibaldi Looks at the Outside World   68

8

Last Thoughts on Politics and War   77

PART TWO
GARIBALDI THROUGH THE EYES OF HIS CONTEMPORARIES

9

In South America, 1836–48   87

10

As a Soldier, Seen by Other Soldiers 96

Colonel Pisacane Criticizes Garibaldi as a Soldier, 1850, *96* Colonel George Cadogan (British Military Attaché) to Lord John Russell (British Minister for Foreign Affairs), October 31, 1859, *100* Marshal MacMahon: An After-Dinner Conversation in Paris, May 24, 1860, *102* Commander Forbes on the Battle of Milazzo, July, 1860, *103* Lieutenant-Colonel Cadolini on the Campaign in Calabria, August, 1860, *106*

11

The Critics: Left, Right, and Center 108

A Critical View by Azeglio, a Conservative Ex-Prime Minister, 1864, *109* A Criticism by Mazzini, 1867, *112* The Views of a Jesuit, After Garibaldi's Defeat at Mentana, 1867, *112* Bakunin and the Socialist International, 1869, *118* Garibaldi Arrives in Southern France, 1870, *120* Garibaldi's Expulsion from the French Assembly at Bordeaux, March 8, 1871, *121* His Departure from Marseilles, February, 1871, *122*

12

Casual Acquaintances 124

Exile in the United States, 1850–51, *125* A Tribute from the French Writer, George Sand, July, 1859, *126* Henry Adams: Report from Palermo, June 9, 1860, *128* Mme. Meuricoffre Writes from Naples, August 1860, *130* A French Novelist Describes Naples After Garibaldi's Departure, November, 1860, *130* John Morley and William Ewart Gladstone on Garibaldi's Visit to England in 1864, *132*

Introduction

Garibaldi has never lacked admirers. During his lifetime he attracted an almost fanatical devotion that was not limited to his fellow countrymen in Italy. For awhile he must have been the most widely known figure in the whole world. Kings and Emperors were afraid of him. Politicians alternately tried to discredit him and then begged for his help. In America and England, just as in Italy, the ordinary working population instinctively recognized him as one of their own kind, appropriated his victories for their own, and hailed his career as promise of a better world to come. Many years later, Jawaharlal Nehru, when studying the life of Garibaldi, realized how the lessons of Italy might apply to India; because the chief message of this life was how an idealistic and unselfish patriotism might triumph over seemingly impossible difficulties and bring a new nation to birth.

If success was one of the ingredients of Garibaldi's popularity, another was failure and the sympathy that failure won him. Certain aspects of his life reveal a lonely and sometimes tragic person. Twice exiled from his own country, he wandered round the world for more than twenty years. Over long periods, he endured severe physical privations and hardships. On three occasions, he was in prison, and once was brutally tortured. He was wounded many times, once sentenced to death in the courts of his own native land, and often had to run for his life with a price on his head. Nevertheless, though fortune often seemed against him, adversity only added to his fascination in the eyes of a world that was agog for romance and heroism.

It was the adventurer and soldier in Garibaldi that mainly exerted this fascination. All his life long, he remained a man of battle, from his first encounter with pirates in the Aegean, to his last campaign against the Grand Army of Bismarck and Moltke. Always, he was to retain something of the pirate in his own make-up, something of the buccaneer and the corsair; and this reflects clearly the imprint of his early career. Ten adventurous years of sailing in the Mediterranean and Black Sea were followed by ten years of exile in South America. In Brazil, he was forced by economic necessity to be-

1

come a professional naval officer and soldier. A man of his temperament was quickly caught up in what he took to be wars of liberation against the oppressive imperialism of Brazil and Argentina. In these wars, he learned to command men and to be a rebel. Here, by trial and error, he acquired the techniques of irregular, guerrilla warfare with which he was later to baffle the armies of Italy, Austria, France, and Germany.

In the tangled, ruthless, political bear garden of South America, he also acquired an abiding suspicion of politics and politicians. There he learned, too, to be and to feel a free man. Never during his long career in public life did Garibaldi submit lightly to conventions and established rules. Nor did he fit smoothly into any regular, military hierarchy. His type of war depended on the formation of a private army of volunteers, whom he recruited from the people of many nations. Among them were always a number of vagabonds and political refugees, very few of whom had ever fought in a regular army; most, like himself, could never have enlisted in any cause that they could not persuade themselves was a war for freedom. Believing strongly in his own personal independence, he also believed in that of others, and this was the only kind of issue that ever aroused his wholehearted and enthusiastic response.

During this period in South America, Garibaldi made a considerable name for himself, and began to win admirers even in distant Europe. But the most important part of his career began in 1848, when, over the age of forty, he was allowed back to Italy. From then on, he devoted his life to the deliverance from Austrian and French occupation of the various states of Italy, and their synthesis in a single nation. In the next twenty-five years, he was to do as much as any man to effect this *risorgimento*, and realize the dream of Italian unity.

Yet Garibaldi remained more than an Italian patriot. His fame and popularity in the rest of the world arose in part from the fact that, though a dedicated nationalist, he did not believe in his country right or wrong, but was simultaneously a convinced internationalist and one of the first campaigners for a united Europe. Empires were wrong, he felt, because they oppressed subject nationalities. Hence, he consistently opposed Pedro in Brazil, Francis Joseph in Austria, and Louis Napoleon in France. Nations, on the other hand, were right, because communities, like individuals, had a just sense of pride and should not be enslaved. But nation states were, as Garibaldi increasingly saw them, only a necessary phase along the path toward a truly international community. At the same time, this man of war developed into something of a pacifist who realized the futility of wars and the need to find a fairer and less wasteful means of international arbitration.

Some thought this was a paradox, and, indeed, many felt that there was a good deal about Garibaldi's beliefs and behavior that was strange, even eccentric. This strangeness was another of the facts about him that caught popular imagination and made him notorious. Although he was in no sense a clever person, his natural sympathy for oppressed minorities provided him with a collection of opinions that were as unfashionable as they were honest and humanitarian. A religious freethinker, a champion of female emancipation, of the equality of man, and of the rights of labor, he was thus a very unusual person for his day. He was equally exceptional in his approval of cremation, vegetarianism, racial equality, and the abolition of capital punishment.

Almost any one of these beliefs would have labelled Garibaldi as individualistic and original in the Italy of 1870. It seemed equally strange that, when he was a colonel and then a general in the Uruguayan and Piedmontese armies, he regularly refused to collect his salary; or that, when he wielded dictatorial powers, he continued to live in the greatest simplicity and would use only a minimum of coercive authority. Never one for the ordinary amenities of civilized life, he preferred to live a poor man, ready to wash and darn his own clothes, to milk his own goats, and till his own land.

His choice of residence was equally nonconformist, for this admirer of Robinson Crusoe decided to build a house, with his own hands, on the deserted island of Caprera—the name means "isle of goats." This was about as remote and inaccessible a place as one could possibly have found anywhere in Italy. Only in such an outlandish and unnatural solitude could he feel truly free. There, far away from the confusions and the rhetoric of human society, he used to meditate on politics, history, and religion. Nor was it surprising that the results of his isolated meditations sometimes came as a shock. From Caprera, he would appear suddenly on the mainland to call his volunteer army into existence for some enterprise that he had not discussed even with his friends.

Whether he was in this island home, or sitting in parliament, or whether he was visiting the British Prime Minister, Garibaldi continued to wear the costume he had habitually worn in South America, the red shirt and grey poncho that lent such a bizarre and even theatrical touch to his appearance. This kind of disdain for the conventions of his time may have seemed, to some observers, trivial, or artificial, or even a crude method of drawing attention to himself; but no one who knew him well, whether friend or foe, accused Garibaldi of ostentatiousness or vainglorious display. His mannerisms were in fact genuine, and they reflected an attitude of mind that in its own way was creative, original, and even important for the society in which he lived. To give one example, his liking for the unexpected was an essential quality in a guerrilla leader, and hence had a necessary part to play in winning the only distinguished military victories of the *risorgimento*.

One aspect of Garibaldi's character that sharply distinguished him from other celebrities of the period was his quite unusual appeal to the common people. No doubt they were drawn to him because he was a rebel and an enemy of tyrants, and because he was a man of extraordinary courage and great sympathy with the poor and the persecuted. They instinctively liked the way in which—unlike some other professed socialists—he renounced the practice by which all visitors to the King of Italy used to exchange their ordinary clothes for a top hat and frock coat. Even when King Victor Emanuel betrayed him and put him in peril of his life, this radical republican never treated the monarch with the almost vulgar outbursts of disrespect that sometimes came from Cavour, the conservative aristocrat; yet he was never obsequious; though he could defer, he was never deferential, and this won him great popular esteem.

Garibaldi's humble origins and way of life provided him with an understanding of ordinary people that was itself one reason for many of his successes. Of the three great pioneers of Italian patriotism, he was not an intellectual, as was Giuseppe Mazzini; he was not a politician to be remotely compared with Camille de Cavour; and yet he was a practical, workaday person, with practical, straightforward aims that could be comprehended by ordinary folk. He alone of the three could speak to both the others, for he would respect the personality even of his enemies. He alone would treat peasant and monarch alike with equal respect and courtesy.

This fact helps to explain the indispensable contribution of Garibaldi to the *risorgimento*. For the cause of Italian nationality meant little or nothing to the great majority of Italians in 1850, and this one man above all was able to bring home to the poorer and less well-educated of his fellow citizens something of what nationality signified. He was much more obviously one of themselves than were the intellectuals and the politicians. They also recognized him as a man of honesty and disinterestedness. A belief was present among the peasants of southern Italy that he was invulnerable and needed only to shake his tunic for bullets to fall harmless at his feet (A. Maffei, *Brigand Life in Italy: a History of Bourbonist Reaction,* London, 1865, Vol. I, 86); and this legend of invincibility was a powerful motive in making people join what must otherwise have seemed a lost cause. Even among the inhabitants of Lombardy, in the much less primitive north, mothers would bring their children for him to bless; and in some villages, his picture was kept framed in the golden shrine of a saint. His striking looks and wonderful voice helped to make some Italians think him a real God who had descended from heaven to redress their wrongs and relieve their sufferings.

Since patriotism was a true religion for Garibaldi, he deliberately exploited his reputation as a magician and miracle worker, in order to neutralize the potential opposition of a strongly religious and conservative peasantry. By persuading even a few of them to take up arms for Italy, and many others to assume at least a benevolent neutrality, he gave Italian patriotism a firm base for the first time. His astonishing conquest of Sicily in 1860 would have been inconceivable without at least the tacit support of great numbers among the common people, and his ability to appeal to them at this decisive moment was not least among his services to Italy. Cavour and the politicians positively feared the effects of allowing popular involvement in the *risorgimento;* that is why Cavour failed when, in an emergency, he had to attempt a revolution in Naples and the Papal States; and that is one reason why so many Italians were disaffected toward the new Kingdom of Italy once it was in existence. Garibaldi, on the other hand, rather feared that, without popular involvement, the *risorgimento* could be perverted to improper ends and might even be morally unjustifiable; what was equally frightening to him was that, without popular support, it might fail.

Garibaldi thus exercised an educative role in Italy, but another invaluable service to his country was the effect he produced abroad. Unlike any other Italian soldier, he earned a very respectful consideration from experienced generals in Austria and Germany. Frenchmen could call him the most dangerous enemy ever encountered by the Emperor Louis Napoleon (Nassau William Senior, *Conversations with Distinguished Persons during the Second Empire, 1860 to 1863,* ed. M.C.M. Simpson, London, 1880, Vol. I, 109).

Baffled by the admiration for Garibaldi in England, Pope Pius IX had to confess that this one man compelled him to keep an army that, in proportion to the population of the Papal States, was the largest in the world (*The Roman Question: extracts from the despatches of Odo Russell*, ed. Noel Blakiston, London, 1962, p. 351).

Much more important, however, than the fear Garibaldi aroused, there was the positive and even decisive support he won from many foreigners for the Italian cause. There were, for example, many excellent Hungarian soldiers in his volunteer army, as well as contingents from a dozen other nations. It is still unknown, and probably always will be, how much money was subscribed abroad to finance his conquest of southern Italy, but it may have been as much as or more than that subscribed in Italy itself. It is also impossible to estimate how much the glamor which attached to this single name helped to quicken the immense enthusiasm elsewhere for the *risorgimento*. Yet, at a time when Cavour and other conservative patriots in Italy were looking on Garibaldi as a dangerous revolutionary who should be suppressed, at a time when upper-class Italians despised him as an uneducated, feather-brained demagogue, there were many liberals and conservatives in other countries who enthusiastically praised not only his military skill but his moral rectitude and common sense.

This admiration was invaluable for Italy at a time when foreign support was important for morale and diplomatically necessary. Abraham Lincoln thought Garibaldi of sufficient stature to offer him a command in the American Civil War. At least one of what could be called his "piratical" enterprises against another "friendly" nation was supported by Lord Palmerston from the British secret service funds (G. B. Henderson, *Crimean War Diplomacy and Other Historical Essays*, Glasgow, 1947, p. 239). To Gladstone and the philanthropist Lord Shaftesbury, he was a person of real worth and integrity, a man who symbolized resurgent Italy and the courageous adventurousness that contributed such an indispensable element to the making of the nation.

Some of these same foreign statesmen were simultaneously antagonized by Cavour's deceitfulness and by the sheer ruthlessness of his plan to create a major world war; yet they were reinforced in their instinctive enthusiasm for the Italian cause when Garibaldi insisted that the issue was one of liberating subject peoples, not one of Italy being "conquered" by Cavour's Kingdom of Piedmont. By stressing that his was a war for freedom and not aggrandizement, and by proving that Italians were ready to fight for their own cause instead of relying like Cavour on French imperialist ambitions, Garibaldi made an essential contribution—one which could have come from no one else. And Cavour, in the end, generously acknowledged the fact.

In February, 1821, Lord Byron had been speculating on the chances of a nationalist revolution in the Italian peninsula. "It is no great matter, supposing that Italy could be liberated, who or what is sacrificed," he wrote: "it is a grand object—the very *poetry* of politics. Only think—a free Italy!!! Why, there has been nothing like it since the days of Augustus" (*The Works of Lord Byron: Letters and Journals*, ed. E. Prothero, London, 1901, Vol. V, 205). The free Italy that he envisaged did not come officially into existence as a nation until March, 1861, and without the work of both Cavour and Garibaldi such a result would hardly have been possible even then. Some people were subsequently able to look back on what had happened as though it were a simple, natural, inevitable fact; yet, until nearly the last moment, Cavour himself had not thought of a unified peninsula as more than a remote possibility. All that he had hoped was to create a strong north-Italian kingdom based on his own state of Piedmont; and most other Italians were not even so advanced in their expectations as that.

Garibaldi, on the other hand (despite the fact that the only Italy he had known was a checkerboard of seven separate and weak states), had for years believed religiously in the existence of an Italian nation. Furthermore, he had the intuitive sense that this could now be practical politics, if only someone had the courage to believe in it and start fighting. Politicians in Italy affected to look down on him as a doctrinaire and a dreamer; but it was he who in fact convinced Cavour that national unification was now feasible in practice.

Far from being just a dreamer, Garibaldi here proved himself to be a hardheaded man of common sense. He saw (as Mazzini never saw) that republicans would have to accept the monarchy and accept the hegemony of Piedmont if Italy was to be made. He was the man who, at a decisive moment in 1860, laid down the program of "Italy and Victor Emanuel"; who, as a result, rallied enough radicals and conservatives to cooperate momentarily with each other; who then acted on his conviction that liberal Europe was bound to support a revolution that had evident popular support; and who finally worked the miracle of selling his program to great numbers of southern Italians who had heard neither of Victor Emanuel nor even of Italy. When, in 1860, the time arrived for a plebiscite on whether or not to form a united nation, some of the peasants insisted that they knew only Garibaldi and wanted to vote for him: their vote, somewhat high-handedly, was registered as affirmative. A few months later, the existence of an Italian nation was officially declared.

Chronology of the Life of Garibaldi

1807	(July 4) Born at Nice (at that time part of France), the son of Domenico Garibaldi, a fisherman and coastal trader.
1814	Nice is once again joined to the Kingdom of Piedmont-Sardinia.
1824–33	Garibaldi lives as a sailor in the Mediterranean and Black Sea.
1832	He acquires his master's certificate as a merchant captain.
1833	In touch with Mazzini's patriotic organization, Young Italy, and visits its headquarters at Marseilles.
1834	As a naval rating in the Piedmontese navy, he takes part in a mutiny for the republican cause. Sentenced to death by default, after escaping to France.
1835	Takes casual jobs in France and with the Bey of Tunis.
1836	Sails for Rio de Janeiro from Marseilles in a 200 ton brigantine.
1836–40	As soldier, corsair, and naval captain, he fights for the break-away province of Rio Grande, in its attempt to free itself from the Brazilian Empire.
1841	He tries his hand at various jobs—including cattle herdsman, trader, and schoolmaster at Montevideo.
1842	Put in command of the small Orientale (Uruguayan) fleet against Manuel de Rosas, the dictator of Argentina.
1843	Also becomes commander of the newly formed Italian Legion at Montevideo.
1846	Wins the "battle" of St. Antonio, after which a sword of honor is subscribed for him in Italy.
1847	Briefly in command of the defense of Montevideo. Offers his services to Pope Pius IX.
1848	(April) Leads eighty of his legionaries back to Italy. (July) Vainly offers to fight for the King of Piedmont. (August) In command of a volunteer unit at Milan against the Austrians, and survives two brisk engagements at Luino and Morazzone.
1849	(February) As an elected deputy in the Roman Assembly (after the flight of the Pope), he proposes the creation of a Roman Republic.

9

(April) As a general of brigade, he beats off an attack by the French at the St. Pancrazio gate of Rome.

(May) Defeats a Neapolitan army at Velletri.

(June) Takes a principal part in defending Rome against further French attacks.

(July) Leads a few thousand men from Rome through central Italy to escape from French and Austrian armies.

(August) After disbanding his men in San Marino, he is chased at sea and on land by the Austrians; his first wife, Anita, dies.

(September) As soon as he arrives back in Piedmontese territory, he is arrested and deported as an undesirable.

1849–50   For seven months in Tangiers, where he writes the first edition of his memoirs.

1850–51   In New York and on Staten Island; he works in a candle factory.

1851–52   Travels to Peru.

1852–53   As a "citizen of Peru," he captains a clipper to the far east, returning to Lima *via* Australia and New Zealand.

1854   Returns by way of New York, carrying a cargo of coal from Newcastle (England) to Genoa.

1855   Engaged to an English lady, Mrs. Emma Roberts.
Buys part of the Island of Caprera, north of Sardinia.

1856   Comes to England on a scheme (largely financed by individual British politicians and British secret service funds) to buy a ship and lead an expedition to release political prisoners in Naples; but the ship is wrecked.

1858   Goes to Turin to meet Count Cavour, the Piedmontese Prime Minister, who wants him to organize a corps of volunteers, in anticipation of another war against Austria.

1859   (April) As a general in the Piedmontese army, he forms this corps, the *Cacciatori delle Alpi,* and war begins.

(May) Takes Varese and Como, while the main Franco-Piedmontese forces are fighting in the plain of Lombardy.

(September) After the armistice of Villafranca, Baron Ricasoli gives him command of the army of Tuscany.

(November) When his project to march into the Papal States is overruled, he returns to civil life.

1860   (April) As deputy for Nice in the Piedmontese parliament at Turin, he attacks Cavour for ceding Nice to Louis Napoleon, Emperor of the French.

(May) He sets out with a thousand volunteers on a piratical raid against the forces of the Neapolitan Bourbons.

After an engagement at Calatafimi, he captures Palermo, the capital of Sicily.

(July) He wins the battle of Milazzo, near Messina.
(August) Crosses the Straits of Messina, eluding the sizable Neapolitan navy.
(September) After a lightning campaign in Calabria, he captures Naples, the largest town in Italy, and makes himself "Dictator of the Two Sicilies."
(October) After a big battle on the Volturno River, he holds plebiscites in Sicily and Naples, and then gives the whole of southern Italy to Cavour, proclaiming Victor Emanuel as King of a united nation.
(November) He returns to Caprera, which now remains permanently his home.

1861　(April) He attacks Cavour in parliament over the latter's ungenerous treatment of the volunteers.
(July) Lincoln offers him a command in the American Civil War, but the offer is declined.

1862　(July) He begins agitating in Sicily for another march on Rome, evidently with some encouragement from the King and Rattazzi, the Prime Minister.
(August) Seriously wounded in a clash with Italian troops at Aspromonte, in Calabria.
(October) After being imprisoned, he is granted an amnesty by the King.

1863　Resigns from parliament because of martial law being applied in Sicily.

1864　Triumphal reception in England.

1866　Leads another volunteer army in a new war against Austria, after which Venice is joined to Italy.

1867　Again attempts a march on Rome, but is beaten by papal and French forces at Mentana, and once again is arrested by the Italian government.

1870　Joins republican France in the Franco-Prussian war, and is made commander of an army in the Vosges.

1879　Comes to Rome in an attempt to organize the parliamentary opposition against Depretis, the Prime Minister.
The Court of Appeal annuls his twenty-year-old marriage to the Marchesina Raimondi, so that he can marry a third wife, Francesca Armosino, by whom he already has several children.

1882　(June 2) Dies at Caprera.

PART ONE

GARIBALDI AS HE SAW HIMSELF

1

His Youth, as Described in the Memoirs

In later years, Garibaldi often filled idle moments by writing his life history; and there exist five different versions of his memoirs. The three earliest of these were published not in Italy but in New York, Hamburg, and Paris, a fact that testifies to his fame abroad. Episodic, and sometimes inaccurate where they can be checked, they tell the greater part of what is known about his youth; they describe his family at Nice and his early life as a sailor. They also tell, though with some obvious reticences, about his rather inauspicious novitiate as a political revolutionary.

Among other incidents, Garibaldi describes in his autobiography how he was once a teacher in Constantinople, and there learned some Greek in his spare time. He says he knew something of Latin too, so he was not quite as uneducated as his detractors used to maintain. His own first language was not Italian but the Provençal dialect of Nice, and for a while he also seems to have spoken French better than Italian: this explains some of the deficiencies of style and language in his later writing. He also learned Spanish during the twelve years he lived in South America as an exile, after being condemned to "ignominious death" by the government of Piedmont. This South American period in his life was one that Garibaldi used to recall with more vividness and more pleasure than almost any other.

PREFACE TO HIS MEMOIRS, JULY 3, 1872 [1]

I have lived a tempestuous life, and, as with most lives, it has been a mixture of good and bad. I feel sure that I have always tried to act for the best both in regard to myself and toward others. If sometimes I have done wrong, certainly it was not with intent. I have always hated tyranny and lies, and am profoundly convinced that these two are the chief causes of the ills and corruption that affect mankind.

I am a republican, since I believe this the best kind of government for honest people, the one most generally desired and least dependent on violence or imposture. But I would not be so intolerant as to want to impose my republicanism on the English, since they are obviously content with the government of Queen Victoria, and popular contentedness makes their kind of government a republic in all but name. Along with republicanism, however, I am more and more convinced of the need for an honest, temporary dictatorship in countries such as France, Spain and Italy. . . .

No doubt many views in this book will seem pessimistic, but perhaps I will be forgiven by those who possess enough patience to read to the end. At the age of sixty-five, after having believed for most of my life in human progress and betterment, it is with a real sense of bitterness that I look back over the misfortunes and corruption of this so-called civilized century.

HE BECOMES A REVOLUTIONARY [2]

I became a member of *Young Italy* [Mazzini's patriotic society] in my earliest youth, for I was a passionate lover of my country and eagerly desired to know what plans were being made for her rebirth. I earnestly sought out any book or article about Italian freedom and any person who had dedicated his life to this cause. The first who spoke seriously to me about the development of our national movement was a young man from Genoa with whom I found myself on a journey to Taganrog [in the Black Sea]. Colum-

[1] *Le memorie di Garibaldi nella redazione definitiva del 1872*, Bologna, 1932, edizione nazionale, Vol. II, 11–13. This and all future quotations from this source are reprinted with the permission of Casa Editrice Licinio Cappelli.

[2] *Garibaldi's Denkwürdigkeiten, nach handschriftlichen Aufzeichnungen desselben* (trans. into German by Elpis Melena from a manuscript which is now lost), Hamburg, 1861, Vol. I, 15–19.

bus himself when he discovered America can scarcely have felt
more excitement than I at meeting someone whose mind was set
upon liberating his country. As soon as he had told me of the thousands working toward this end, I had found my aim in life. I threw
myself wholeheartedly into the national struggle and made it my
own.

On another journey, when I was sailing with the ship *Clorinda,*
I fell in with a group of Saint-Simonians [French Utopian Social-
ists] who were on their way to Constantinople under the leadership
of Emile Barrault. I got to know this man and told him about the
work of the Italian patriots. He in exchange initiated me into the
ideas of the Saint Simonian sect about which I knew absolutely
nothing. Nor were these talks with Barrault without influence on
the development of my own ideas. The essentially cosmopolitan
outlook of such people showed me the onesidedness of my national
feeling and lifted my eyes beyond mere patriotism and toward the
larger cause of humanity.

In the year 1833 I returned from the east and came to Marseilles.
This was just after several conspiracies had been betrayed to the
various governments of northern and central Italy. Spies had been
able to infiltrate the conspirators, and the Piedmontese police were
in full pursuit. After many arrests had been made, sixty-seven
people were condemned to savage punishments by the military tri-
bunals, and twelve executions were carried out. But the blood of
these martyrs aroused a desire for revenge, and Mazzini decided to
launch a new movement.

The consequent armed incursion from Switzerland into Savoy
was, as everyone knows, brought to nothing because of the incapac-
ity and cowardice of Ramorino. Another movement had been
planned to take place simultaneously, and in this I too had a hand.
At Marseilles I had been friendly with a certain man named Covi,
and he introduced me to Mazzini, assuring him that I could
be trusted. I then joined the Piedmontese navy as a first-class rating
on the frigate *Eurydice.* My instructions were to make proselytes
among the crew. If the movement succeeded, I and my comrades
were to bring this ship over to the republican cause.

My propaganda on the *Eurydice* succeeded, but in my zeal I was
not content with such a minor task. In the port of Genoa, where we
lay at anchor, I heard that an insurrection was due to take place,
and an attack would be made on the police barracks in the Piazza
Sarzana. So, leaving the capture of the frigate to my comrades, I

rowed ashore just before the time agreed for the outbreak and landed on the customs quay. Thence I hastened to the Piazza Sarzana.

I waited about an hour, but nothing happened. A crowd then began to gather, and people were saying that all had failed. Arrests were taking place and the republicans were in flight. As I had entered the Piedmontese navy just to promote this republican revolt, there was no point in returning to my ship, and obviously my duty was to escape too. When troops began to surround the Piazza there was no more time for delay. So I explained my sorry situation to a lady who ran a fruitstall. This good woman, without a second thought, hid me in a back room and procured me some peasant clothes. At seven in the evening of February 5, 1834, I left Genoa through the Lanterna gate in my rustic disguise. I was now an outlaw.

IN SOUTH AMERICA[3]

The sight which met my eyes for the first time, when I reached the top of the barrancas, is really worth recording. The vast undulating plains of Uruguay present a landscape entirely new to a European, and more particularly to an Italian, accustomed from childhood to a country where every inch of ground is covered with houses, hedges, or other labor of man's hands. Here there is nothing of the kind; the Creoles keep the surface of the country exactly as it was left by the natives whom the Spaniards exterminated. . . .

What a handsome fellow is the stallion of the Pampas! His lips have never winced at the iron bit, and his glossy back, never crossed by a rider, shines like a diamond in the sun. His flowing, uncombed mane floats over his flanks when, assembling in his pride the scattered mares, or flying from human pursuit, he outruns the wind. His unshod hoofs, unpolluted by the stable, are white and polished as ivory; and his silky tail, an ample defense against insect attacks, streams behind him in the wind of the Pampas. He is a true sultan of the desert.

Who can conceive the feelings awakened in the heart of a buccaneer of twenty-five by his first sight of that untamed nature? Today —December 20, 1871—bending with stiffened limbs over the fire, I recall with emotion those scenes of the past, when life seemed to

[3] *Autobiography of Giuseppe Garibaldi,* trans. A. Werner, London, 1889, Vol. I, 30–32, 92–93.

smile on me, in the presence of the most magnificent spectacle I
ever beheld. . . .

Among the many vicissitudes of my stormy life, I have not wanted
happy moments; and such, paradoxical though it appears, was the
one when, at the head of a few men, the survivors of many battles,
who had honestly earned the name of heroes, I rode along with the
woman of my heart beside me, throwing myself into a career which,
even more than the sea, had an immense attraction for me. What
mattered it to me that I had no clothes except those I stood up in?
or that I served a poor Republic which could pay not one penny?
I had a sword and carbine, which I carried before me across the saddle. Anita was my treasure, and no less zealous than myself for the
sacred cause of nations, and for a life of adventure. She looked upon
battles as a pleasure, and the hardships of camp-life as a pastime; so
that, however things might turn out, the future smiled on us, and
the vast American deserts which unrolled themselves before our
gaze seemed all the more delightful and beautiful for their wild-
ness. Besides all this, I could feel that I had honestly done my duty
in the various perils which I had been called to share, and had
earned the respect of the warlike sons of Rio Grande.

2
War Against Austria and France

When Garibaldi returned from South America, in 1848, he found Italy still divided into seven small, independent states. Nice, his home town, belonged to the Kingdom of Piedmont-Sardinia, which was ruled by Charles Albert (and after 1849 by Victor Emanuel). Bordering on Piedmont to the east was Lombardy and then Venice, both of them Italian in speech, but both part of the Austrian empire. To the southeast was the Grand Duchy of Tuscany, below which the Papal States (governed by Pope Pius IX) stretched from sea to sea and cut Italy in two.

Garibaldi arrived home just when an insurrection against the Austrians had broken out in part of Lombardy. When the Piedmontese supported this insurrection, he offered Charles Albert his support, but was turned down and had to watch while the badly trained and badly led forces of Piedmont were soundly defeated. Then, with a few volunteers, and in the face of every discouragement from the Piedmontese, who now made peace, he began an independent partisan war of his own against the massive army of Marshal Radetzky, and emerged with some credit from several small engagements; but his hopes of starting a general rebellion proved illusory. He therefore took his men southward to Rome, where another revolution had temporarily overthrown the Pope's government. He played a leading part in the defense of the Roman republic against a French invasion.

GARIBALDI DECLARES PERSONAL WAR ON THE AUSTRIANS IN LOMBARDY, AUGUST 13, 1848 [1]

Italians! In the name of God and the people, I have been elected by the citizens of Milan and their representatives to be a

[1] Enrico Emilio Ximenes, *Epistolario di Giuseppe Garibaldi*, Milan, 1885, Vol. I, 19–20.

leader, a *Duce*. Our aim is to make Italy independent. I therefore cannot accept the humiliating armistice made [on August 9] by the King of Piedmont with the hated foreign Power which dominates our country. The King does not scruple to preserve his crown at the price of cowardice and defeat, but I and my companions are not prepared to buy our lives with such infamy. We will accept any sacrifice to prevent our own sacred land from being trampled by the tyrant who now violates it.

SPEECH TO THE PEOPLE OF VARESE, AUGUST 18, 1848 [2]

It is not with shouts or with applause that we should fight the enemies of our country, but with weapons and the shedding of blood. Every conceivable offensive weapon, whether a gun, a dagger, a scythe, a stick, everything should be utilised in our war against these contemptible assassins from Austria. It is not a question of directly combating the compact and ordered units of an army in the field, but rather of molesting the enemy in every possible way, even on the smallest scale. We must always take them unawares. We must never flag.

Remember, citizens, that every "Croat" you kill is one piece of obscenity the less in Italy [there were Slav units in the Austrian army]. Whoever has a weapon and can wield it, yet refuses to fight, is a coward. And whoever tries to stop you using that weapon for the defense of your fatherland is a traitor.

GARIBALDI ADDRESSES THE CONSTITUENT ASSEMBLY
AT ROME, FEBRUARY 5, 1849 [3]

GARIBALDI. Not only the people of Rome but those of all Italy are looking to us to choose a new form of government, and I therefore propose that we should not leave this hall before we have reached agreement. Let us not bother about mere forms and protocol, for it is nothing less than the destinies of the entire Italian nation which are at issue.

THE SPEAKER. I am not defending procedural forms for their own sake, but I do think we ought to begin by setting up a proper organization for this Assembly before we begin discussion.

[2] *Edizione Nazionale degli Scritti di Giuseppe Garibaldi*, Bologna, 1934, Vol. IV, 94–95.

[3] *Le Assemblee del Risorgimento: Roma*, Rome, 1911, Vol. III, 22–23.

GARIBALDI. These are secondary matters and can come later. The question today is a vital one of principle. To delay one minute would be a crime so long as a third of the Italian nation lies in slavery. Can you not hear the groan of despair which comes from a million Italian throats? And meanwhile we are asked to go on discussing mere forms! I believe profoundly that, now the papal system of government is at an end, what we need in Rome is a republic (*Applause mixed with an occasional sign of disapproval*). Can it be said that the descendants of the ancient Romans are not fit to constitute a Republic? As some people in this body evidently take offense at this word, I reiterate "Long live the republic!"

APPEAL TO THE GOVERNORS OF ROME, APRIL 1, 1849 [4]

Some of you know part of my life history, but not in detail; and so, since it is important to counter the influence of those garrulous military theorists of whom unfortunately we have too many in Italy, let me be immodest. In a hundred engagements I have never been defeated. In my long life as a soldier, have you ever heard a single accusation against me of cowardice or lack of skill? Sometimes I have been called pirate, smuggler or guerrilla, because such epithets are deliberately used to defame a feared rival, and the fact is that again and again I have had to fight against hundreds, against thousands, and beat them. I am absolutely sure that I know how to lead any number of men and make them fight. I am not asking you for command of the whole Roman army. What I would like is permission to leave Rome and be given full powers so as to be able to conscript people in the countryside and organize any fighting units we may find still in existence anywhere in central and northern Italy. . . .

Whatever people say about me, please remember that I have reason to think that I know something about war, and there are facts to support my claim. Furthermore I enjoy some prestige with the populations of Umbria, Romagna, Tuscany, Liguria. I am already known there, and I also have soldiers at Bologna and in Lombardy who could help us in starting a revolution. We may not do great things, but at least we shall raise the spirits of those who have been driven to despair by the defeat of the Piedmontese army.

[4] Ermanno Loevinson, *Giuseppe Garibaldi e la sua legione nello stato Romano, 1848–1849*, Rome, 1907, Vol. III, 58–60.

TWO LETTERS TO HIS WIFE, ANITA[5]

April 19, 1849. I write to say that I am well. I now have to go off with my column to Anagni, arriving probably tomorrow, but how long we are to stay I do not know. We shall find muskets and clothes there. But I shall not be happy until I hear that you arrived safely at Nice. Do write at once. I must hear your news, my very dear Anita. Tell me, too, what you think of events in Genoa and Tuscany. You strong, generous woman, with what contempt you must look on this hermaphrodite generation of Italians! So often have I tried to make them worthy of you, little though they deserve it. Treason has paralyzed our every courageous impulse, so that we are dishonored and the name of Italy will be held up to scorn by foreigners everywhere. I am ashamed to belong to a family which contains so many cowards. And yet I am not discouraged. Nor do I doubt the ultimate destiny of my country. I am even becoming more hopeful, for we now know who the traitors are. They can bring dishonor on an individual without being punished, but not on a whole nation. The heart of Italy is still beating. . . .

June 21, 1849. We are fighting here on the Janiculan hill, and these citizens of Rome are now proving worthy of their past greatness. "Long live the Republic" is the cry with which people endure the pain of amputation and even death itself. One hour of life here in Rome is worth a century of normal existence. How happy my mother should be for giving me life in this wonderful period of Italian history.

THE DEFEAT OF ROME, JUNE, 1849[6]

When the defense could no longer hold out in Rome, it was decided that Garibaldi should lead a sortie. The principal aim was to reach the Adriatic sea and help to relieve Venice, which was under siege from the Austrians. But up in the Abruzzi mountains, he was surrounded by an Austrian force; and then, in the course of a brilliant escape through the enemy patrols, he had to watch Anita die, that Creole Amazon who had become his wife in South America. Some of the narrative of the retreat from Rome is here told by two eyewitnesses.

[5] Ermanno Loevinson, *Giuseppe Garibaldi e la sua legione nello stato Romano, 1848–1849,* Rome, 1907, Vol. III, 75, 106.

[6] Giuseppe Gabussi, *Memoire per servire alla storia della rivoluzione degli*

Our third line of defense was giving way, and Mazzini when he spoke to the General Staff found most of them despondent. So he went to the Assembly and said: "The French have now overrun our second line, but we have not lost the day. Our resistance can still continue as before, since the citizens of Rome are stout-hearted as ever." If things should come to the worst, he added,

> there would be three possibilities left, either capitulation, or a final war of barricades in the street; or else for the army, the Assembly and the government to rely on popular support and leave Rome so as to raise the standard of the republic elsewhere. I myself think capitulation impossible. Of the other two possibilities, the assembly will have to decide, but I prefer the last.

When Mazzini spoke of continuing resistance, Bartolucci shook his head in dissent, and showed those near him a letter from Garibaldi which spoke in a very different sense. When urged by Gabussi to tell people the true state of affairs, he explained to the Assembly that further fighting was impossible. Some voices were then raised to accuse Mazzini of concealing the truth and trying to deceive the deputies. The latter became obviously worried, but said nothing further, and Garibaldi was sent for.

Wrapped in his cloak, sweating profusely and covered with dust, Garibaldi slowly moved forward to speak. His face was composed. When the loud burst of applause had subsided, and the Speaker asked him to tell us the true state of affairs, he confirmed what Bartolucci had said.

> Our former plan of defense is no longer workable. The only hope of continuing the war would be to fall back behind the Tiber River, evacuating the population from the Trastevere and blowing up the bridges. The situation might well have been better had the war been under more positive direction. Yet though errors had been committed, this is no time for recriminations but for prompt and resolute decision.

When asked how long the line of the Tiber could be held, Garibaldi answered "for a few days only." He also thought that Mazzini's second proposal for street fighting was out of the question, since:

> the French will never involve themselves in a war of barricades: they already command the hills and can bombard Rome at will. Bombardment will break the morale of citizens, for they are only human, and we would have difficulty keeping order. I prefer Mazzini's last proposal, for us all to leave Rome and turn the war rather against the Austrian forces to the north.

He then looked at the deputies with his usual winning smile and added:

> but remember gentlemen, you will find life much more uncomfortable in the countryside, with none of your comfortable houses, no cafés, and no regular meals. You will often have to sleep under an open sky, and sometimes in the rain. You will have to march in the burning heat of the sun, and there will be no carriages. We shall eat what we can get, if necessary our horses. So think carefully, and decide at once, because I can hold out against the French only for a few hours longer. As for myself, I have decided.

With these words Garibaldi left the hall. . . .

As soon as he had gone, the discussion began. Capitulation was ruled right out, even without any debate. As to continuing the fight on this side of the Tiber, that was thought too great a sacrifice to force on people. Only the citizens of Rome themselves were entitled to go down fighting under the ruins of their city if they chose, and evidently this was not their wish. The remaining possibility, to leave Rome, was chiefly championed by Mazzini and Sterbini, but in a heated discussion there were heard strong arguments against the wisdom of pitting ourselves against four different armies [French, Austrian, Spanish, and Neapolitan] when our forces were exhausted and lacking munitions. . . . Those who were against leaving Rome were easily in the majority.

A SWISS OFFICER DESCRIBES THE RETREAT
FROM ROME, JULY, 1849 [7]

July 2, 1849. A large and applauding crowd surrounded the remnants of our valiant army as we left Rome. I and ten other

[7] Gustav von Hoffstetter, *Tagebuch aus Italien, 1849*, Zürich, 1851, pp. 318–67, 432–37.

mounted soldiers were the rearguard, and we were the last through the gates. It was a bitter moment. Repeatedly I had to look back at the towers and palaces of the eternal city, unconsciously halting my mettlesome horse. But finally I mastered my inner feelings and gave Moretto his head. Soon I overtook Garibaldi who was galloping up and down the column urging them to make better speed.

We continued uninterruptedly and in complete silence from 10 p.m. till 7:00 the next morning. No smoking was allowed, and orders were given in a whisper. This speed and stealth were designed by the general to give us a good start and take us quickly into the mountains. Our mounted patrols coursed along the right flank, and a mounted advanced guard sometimes cantered several miles ahead.

July 3. By 7 a.m. we had reached the hills, and there we were met by the cheering population of Tivoli. The troops here found food already prepared, for at two in the morning the general had sent an officer and a detachment of horse ahead for this purpose. . . .

Our cavalry was at first commanded by Major Müller and Major Migliazzo. They were four hundred strong, almost all ex-dragoons. Later they were placed under Colonel Bueno, a South American whom I was to find frivolous and self-willed. They had good horses, but lacked equipment. Untrained, and without the necessary accoutrements, they could hardly have stood up to a charge by regular cavalry, and yet they were indispensable for procuring food supplies promptly as we continued our march. They also took over most of the burdensome job of security and espionage. Without this cavalry unit, we should have had to feel our way through the mobile columns of Austrian and French troops, and sometimes to fight just to obtain information. Our artillery consisted of one small field piece and gun carriage drawn by four horses. If any city showed itself hostile, there was a real advantage in being able to terrify it with a couple of shots. Moreover it was useful to make the enemy think that we had artillery with us. . . .

We had paper money to pay the troops and find provisions, but only enough for four weeks. In Tuscany, moreover, this Roman paper money had no legal currency, and hence Garibaldi changed it into coin in the bigger towns such as Terni and Todi. The depreciation of this paper money meant a sizable loss to these communities later. . . .

July 4. Yesterday we marched for one and a half hours southwards to make it seem as though Garibaldi were taking that direction. At dusk we suddenly turned right across the fields, and at midnight bivouacked near some water. Once again we were not far from Tivoli, hidden in a fold of the ground. Our shrewd general always managed to deceive the enemy with such movements all along our perilous route. No third party apart from him and myself knew where any march would end. Often even I did not know what we would do next.

I had control of security and made some very simple rules. Ahead of us and behind, when on main roads, I kept mounted units up to three or four miles away. On each side of us would be several detachments of either infantry or cavalry according to the kind of land . . . Some of our mounted troops would often remain behind for an hour or two after we had left. The baggage if possible we would send on an hour ahead of time with a special guard. Very rarely did we light fires at night.

Usually we had two marches, one from 2 a.m. till 10 a.m., the other from 5:00 in the evening until 8:00, or even as late at 10 o'clock. In between whiles we camped in some shady and well-watered place. Food was ready by 2:00 at the latest, so that we could start off again at 5:00. Many times our second march lasted well into the night, and my own job became very laborious as a result. Bread could not be obtained every day, but we rarely lacked wine or meat. The meat we used to roast, using a green branch as a spit. We had no fat or salt, yet this American-style food was extremely tasty.

July 5. . . . This evening at 7:00 we had a review of the day's march, and Garibaldi gave a brief but pithy talk to his men.

July 6. After our pack animals and baggage had left at midnight, the rest of the column began at 2:30 a.m., and we had an excellent day's march. The general's words had worked wonders. The soldiers feared him as much as they loved him. They knew very well that he was capable of having them shot without even waiting to take the cigar out of his mouth. He knew only two punishments, either a reprimand, or death. . . .

July 7. During the defense of Rome I had often had occasion to admire Garibaldi's sure hand in directing a battle and his quick and sure eye for detail. Now I was able to observe each day his exceptional skill in matters of security and intelligence. He had acquired this ability in long years of warfare with quickly-moving light troops. I probably had here a master with no superior in the world. His energy was boundless. Whenever we left camp he first found guides and then gave instructions to those officers whose job it was to procure information about enemy movements or to provide food for the day's journey. It was my task to supervise the departure of the main column, and in the meantime he and his wife rode up to the advance guard with any requisite instructions. Often he moved several miles ahead so that we should have plenty of time to deploy or to take evasive action against the enemy. Small or large detachments were sent at his orders to protect our flank. Frequently he would ride back to the rearguard so as to check how the whole column was moving. . . .

July 10. Some people might think that the adventurousness of our way of life and the very uniqueness of our situation would have fostered a certain familiarity between the officers and Garibaldi, but in practice this never happened, not even with his own trusted companions who had fought with him in America, men such as Marochetti and Sacchi; even these still approached him with the greatest respect, and any one of them would call himself happy if the general addressed them with a friendly—one might almost say a gracious—word. Any advice, any good idea from whatever quarter, was always welcome, though any over-insistent remark fell on deaf ears. Disobedience, or even any disregard of his orders, I never saw even once. The hot-blooded Italian soldiers were easily pacified by his rock-like calm. Garibaldi, as many people have said before, was born to command. His exceptional frugality, his tough physique, the fiery ardor of his own country, together with the unshakable equanimity of mind which he learned in America, these combined to give him an authority over his men which made any feat look possible. . . .

July 11. The failure of the enemy to comprehend our movements must have been increased all the more by the skill with which Garibaldi directed our marches. Never starting at the same hour; sudden changes of direction; one march today, two tomorrow; leaving our rearguard stationary behind us; suddenly moving on to a main road, only to abandon it an hour later; unexpectedly long stretches of marching combined with three or four small ones; roudabout detours where a short cut would have been possible; spreading false information, for example rations being ordered for as many as 6,000 men—all these were part of his game. Even our method of pitching camp, in all appearance so strange and disorganized, was intended to give the local population a false idea of our strength. Hardly ever did Garibaldi quarter us in cities or villages, and this too contributed not a little to lay a false trail.

Not only were our marches irregular, but so were our security procedures. The advance posts were never disposed in the same way twice. Today we would have a couple, but tomorrow three whole companies would be used, and then the day after just one. In one situation he would make a great show of using large units, in another he kept them concealed, and sometimes a few weak mounted patrols were the only guard we had. So doing, the Austrians were deceived and made cautious, and it was the easier for us to elude them.

Today, July 11, Garibaldi decided to form additional small groups of partisans in order to deceive the enemy. Cucelli was sent with one company towards Perugia, Amero with another towards Foligno, while Isnardi took his men in the direction of Orvieto. They had orders to move quickly, yet prudently, to take prisoners and get information, acting in every way as partisan bands. The final orders from Garibaldi were that their safety lay essentially in often changing position, so that they never should spend the whole of any one night in the same place. . . .

July 14. [Near Orvieto] Garibaldi's friendly words persuaded one person to trust us and act as our guide. This reassured another group of shepherds who came up to us so as to satisfy their curiosity. With such people the general can behave in a way which always gets excellent results. In a few minutes they are all trying to outdo him in courtesy and telling him all they know about the enemy and his intentions. I remember he used to say: "What are you afraid of? Am I speaking German to you? Are we robbing you and setting fire to your property? Are we fighting for you or against you? Are we not your own compatriots?"

When we returned, the troops were already preparing food. They had killed several oxen from our flock, and we obtained bread from Todi; but today there was no wine. One soldier was caught stealing a chicken from a woman in this poor village, and has been executed today. As the shots rang out, Garibaldi rose and said to the astonished troops who did not know what had happened: "This is the way I punish thieves! Are we fighting for freedom, or are we just robbers? Are we here to protect people or to oppress them?" There were shouts from the soldiers of *Evviva Garibaldi*, and I am sure the loudest shouts came from those who had just been eating a stolen chicken themselves.

Unfortunately it was every day more obvious that not the best people of the Roman army had joined our column, and that the morale and discipline of our men was not improved by such a circuitous means of progress. There were only two remedies: either we had to retrace our steps, or else hurry forward to the coast and give our troops some tangible hope. . . .

The inhabitants [of Orvieto] shut their doors against us and sent a deputation to forbid our entry. They were ready, however, to give us as much wine, bread and meat as we wanted. The general sent this deputation back to the town without deigning to address them a single word. . . .

July 31. The Republic of San Marino lies on an immense outcrop of rock rising perpendicularly from the plain. . . . Officers and men all pressed forward to admire such a magnificent sight. The general posted our rearguard here, and then led his column, now only 1,800 strong, into the narrow valley which separated us from the rock and this independent republic. Meanwhile the cavalry were ordered into San Marino territory on the far side of the valley, an illegality which tactical considerations forced on us. He himself with a few companions then climbed up toward the city.

The government of San Marino at once agreed to let us fall back on their territory and to give us food. As we returned to the main column, we heard some shots, and despite the dangerous and stony path we rushed back at full speed. They were in full flight, followed by several companies of Austrian troops through the ravine which runs round the great rock of San Marino and emerges on the road to Rimini. As we reached the slope, we recognized Anita, the General's wife; she alone was trying to end the panic, cracking her whip and shouting at them to stop. Not one of her companions had the courage to stand with her. Quickly she joined Garibaldi, and, furious at this cowardly flight, led our column toward the city. . . .

Obviously there was nothing more to be done with troops who were worn out by marches and fatigue. Their boots were mostly in tatters. Most of the officers were fed up with a war which offered so little hope, and their horses and mules were exhausted. It seemed much better to go back home than to fall into an inevitable captivity. The general, moreover, would be personally safer without soldiers, since clearly he could no longer count on them in an encounter with the enemy, and yet he could not honorably desert them.

So he put his position to the representatives of the San Marino government, telling them he was ready to lay down his arms so long as the Austrians would promise to let his men go home in peace. An envoy of the government then took this proposal to the Austrian commander.

Meanwhile Garibaldi published the following order:

> San Marino, 31 July 1849. We have found a refuge here and must behave as well as possible to our hosts. We shall then deserve the kind of consideration which is due to helpless refugees. I now release my companions from any obligation toward me, leaving them free to return to private life. But I remind them that Italy must not be allowed to remain in her present shameful state, and that it is better to die than to live as a slave of some foreign Power.
>
> Garibaldi.

At first the Austrians refused to treat, but that evening they requested a parley with the general. Garibaldi did not accept, preferring that the representatives of San Marino should make a truce in his name, for he was sure they would do their best to obtain good conditions.

Our enterprise, which had begun in the Roman Republic, was about to end in the Republic of San Marino. I hope that the reasons for our insuccess will by now be clear to everyone who knows about military matters. For thirty days our column of three or four thousand men had fought continuously. We had had no base of operation and no territory which could offer us an even momentary refuge. There was now almost no further hope of success, and so we had no option but to dissolve. After we had undergone continuous marches by day and night, the enemy columns were beginning to close in on us. . . . Every day our numbers grew fewer, every day morale weakened, and even officers were absconding. . . . Before Garibaldi formally released his soldiers, the column had in fact disintegrated.

3
First Move Toward a United Italy

The Piedmontese government claimed that Garibaldi, by fighting for the revolution at Rome, had again lost his rights as a Piedmontese citizen, so they now exiled him a second time. First he lived in North Africa, then in the United States. Eventually forced back to his trade as a sea captain, he carried cargoes of copper from Chile, and of guano and wool from Peru. Early in the 1850's, he sailed round the world in command of a 400 ton clipper. When allowed to return home, he used his savings to buy half the island of Caprera, just off Sardinia. Here, he lived by farming and fishing, but so long as the Austrians still dominated the Italian peninsula his thoughts were of how to prepare another war of liberation against them. He now cut adrift from Mazzini and the other uncompromising republicans, for in his judgment the best chance of success would be to coerce the Piedmontese monarchy into challenging Austria once again.

GARIBALDI'S PROGRAM FOR ITALY, circa 1855 [1]

To make *a single Italy* must be our first goal. The Italian peninsula is made up of small states: there is Tuscany as well as Piedmont; there are some Italians who owe loyalty to the Pope, others who acknowledge the Bourbons [of Naples], others who are republicans, and others look to Murat [French Pretender to Southern Italy]. Besides these there are some other even smaller groups who, however negligible, cannot help but damage the concept of

[1] *Garibaldi, Vittorio Emanuele, Cavour, nei fasti della patria, documenti inediti,* ed. Giacomo Emilio Curàtulo, Bologna, 1911, p. 24.

national unity. All these elements must amalgamate and join whoever is strongest among them, or else they will be destroyed;
there is no middle way. The most substantial element in Italy I take
to be the Piedmontese, and I therefore advise that all should gather
round them. We should be ready to accept a rigorous dictatorship
from Piedmont as a means of emancipating ourselves from foreign
domination.

LETTER TO JESSIE WHITE MARIO, FEBRUARY 3, 1856 [2]

If I were sure of being joined by a reasonable number of people, even with only a small chance of success, can you doubt that I
should joyfully try once again to realize the main idea of my whole
life, even if an atrocious death awaited me? If you think otherwise,
you cannot know me at all. I can say, proudly but without vainly
boasting, that I will stand alongside the very staunchest of Italian
patriots. My past history is there to prove it, and to be able to fight
for Italy would in my estimation be paradise. Wife, children, the
comforts of life—none of these will hold me back when our holy
cause is at stake.

I will say even more. Though I disapprove of Mazzini's policy of
insurrections, they would have had one follower the more if I had
ever found myself on the spot at the time. If I do not put myself up
as leader of one of these insurrections, it is only because I see no
probability of success, and you know enough of me to realize that
I have some experience of daring enterprises.

One word about Piedmont. The Piedmontese have an army of
40,000 men and an ambitious king [Victor Emanuel]. In cooperation with them we might really start something and succeed, and
that is what most Italians have now convinced themselves. On the
other hand, if Piedmont hesitates or falls short of our expectations,
we shall repudiate her. If others should prove to be the ones who
start this holy war, I shall be with them however foolhardy they
may be. All I ask is that there is a genuine and serious movement.
If you fight, I shall be with you [Jessie White was a close friend of
Mazzini]. But I will not risk making Italians a laughing stock by
supporting an utterly useless rebellion.

[2] Enrico Emilio Ximenes, *Epistolario di Giuseppe Garibaldi*, Milano, 1885,
Vol. I, 48–49.

FELICE FORESTI TO GIORGIO PALLAVICINO, FEBRUARY 22, 1857 [3]

Garibaldi is here in Genoa, and sends you his heartfelt greetings. We have twice had dinner together and we spoke a great deal about Italy. We also talked of you whom he rightly regards as one of the best Italians [Pallavicino was also in touch with King Victor Emanuel]. What he said to me was this:

> If the Piedmontese king is truly ready to put himself at the head of the Italian revolution, he must cautiously but fearlessly help those real patriots who are ready to act. I have a plan which you should pass on to Pallavicino. The Piedmontese government is going to sell three steamships by public auction. The patriotic party ought to buy these and hand them over to brave and trusty captains who are normally engaged in commerce and so would not arouse suspicion. These ships should then be used for trading in the Mediterranean, or else we could lease them to the Rubattino or some other shipping company. In either case we should get a good and safe monetary return, but at the same time the ships would be fully equipped for fighting, with eager and warlike crews ready for the first sign of revolution. Such a revolution will probably start in Sicily or Naples, and my plan is that we northerners ought to be ready to go at once to support it. But the Piedmontese government ought to help us by meeting some of the initial costs of purchase.

DR. BERTANI TELLS OF GARIBALDI'S DEAL WITH THE PIEDMONTESE [4]

One fine day [in December, 1858] Garibaldi entered my consulting room with a radiant face and a voice broken with emotion as he embraced me. "At last they have agreed to act," he said. "I have been empowered at the very highest level [in a meeting with Cavour, the Piedmontese Prime Minister] to tell our friends to get ready. We must all stay closely together if we are going to make Italy, and hence I count on you." As I congratulated him, I asked whether we would have to rely on French help; and he answered

[3] *Daniele Manin e Giorgio Pallavicino, epistolario politico (1855–1857)*, ed. B. E. Maineri, Milan, 1878, pp. 363–64.

[4] Agostino Bertani, "I cacciatori dell'Alpi," *Il Politecnico, repertorio mensile di studi*, Milan, 1860, Vol. VIII, 290–91.

that the more there were of us, the fewer Frenchmen would be needed.

Then he told me about the conversations he had had in government circles at Turin and of his complete confidence in the army, with a lot else too. To such a simple, generous soul, the mere announcement of such an enterprise was a guarantee that the means provided would be sufficient. He had had enough of the vain projects of earlier years and now put his whole trust in this new scheme, considering Cavour's promises to be a pledge of action on a vast and certain scale. All the hopes which had so often been dashed in the past now flooded back, and he had a greater confidence than ever in the capability of a nation in arms. In his mind's eye he already envisaged battalions of citizens moving forward with irresistible impetus, and he saw Italy redeemed largely by her own hands. He kept on repeating that we must all be united and all must take arms if we were going to succeed on our own.

RECOLLECTION OF THE CAMPAIGN OF 1859[5]

Cavour, the Prime Minister of Piedmont, appointed Garibaldi a general in charge of a special volunteer corps, and the long-anticipated war of liberation began in April, 1859. But it soon became clear to Garibaldi that the conservatives mainly wanted to exploit his popularity and prevent him fighting the kind of private war that he had favored in 1848-1849. The regular army detested the volunteers and made life as difficult for them as possible. When told that they would have to sign on for eight years, many of them preferred to go home.

After a few days' stay at Turin [in April, 1859], where I was to perform the service of enlisting Italian volunteers, I soon perceived with whom I had to deal and what was wanted of me. I chafed at it, but what was to be done? Nothing but accept the lesser evil, and, while unable to do all the good I wished, to obtain what little could be obtained for our unhappy country.

Garibaldi was to keep out of sight; to appear and disappear when

[5] *Autobiography of Giuseppe Garibaldi*, trans. A. Werner, London, 1889, Vol. II, 71–98.

wanted. The volunteers ought to know that he was at Turin, so that they might be attracted to the standards; but at the same time Garibaldi was to be requested to hide himself, to give no umbrage to diplomacy. What a condition! To summon the volunteers in large numbers, but to command only a small proportion of them, and those the least fit to carry arms! The volunteers assembled, but were not allowed to see me. Depots were formed at Cuneo and Savigliano, while I was banished to Rivoli, near Susa. . . .

General Lamarmora, the minister of war, who had always been averse to the enrollment of the volunteers, refused to recognize the rank of my officers, so that, in order to give some nominal legality to these rejected ones, recourse was had to the subterfuge of issuing commissions signed by the minister of the interior, and not by his excellency of war. Yet we submitted to it all in silence. . . . It was the old grievance, begun at Milan in 1848 by Sobrero; continued at Rome [1849] by Campello, who decreed that the corps commanded by me was never to exceed the number of 500; and [now] completed by Cavour, who limited me to 3000.

The three regiments were composed of six battalions, with 600 men in each, forming a total of 3600; but the formation of the depots, and the fact that my raw levies were unused to marching, reduced their numbers to 3000 before we had crossed the Ticino.

The King, who was certainly better than the men who surrounded him in 1859, sent a second order to march towards Lago Maggiore, and operate on the Austrian right. This was perhaps displeasing to the court cabal; not so to me, who thenceforward found myself free to act—a position to me worth millions. I therefore took leave of my brave old general [Cialdini]—to whom, short as our acquaintance had been, I was already united by true affection —and marched to Chivasso, and thence to Biella. The brilliant and sympathetic reception given to my men by the people of Biella was a good omen. We remained a day or two in that friendly city, and then marched on to Gattinara.

The enemy, posted at Novara, having heard that I was marching in that direction, sent about twenty soldiers to cut off the ferry over the Sesia; but an outpost of ours, stationed at that point, prevented this movement.

Here it may not be beside the point to mention an incident very discreditable to us Italians, which should never have been allowed by the people to occur. It is true that the system of terror adopted by the Austrians in Italy had completely cowed the population;

while for Cavour's plan of disarming the national guards on the frontiers, no words of condemnation are strong enough. If, therefore, there were manifestations of weakness on the part of our peasants, or of insolence on that of the tyrants from beyond the Alps—who have so long believed themselves absolute masters of our affairs, our property, and our persons—this was only what might have been expected. Preceded by the terror which they knew how to strike into the inhabitants, these lords of Italy extorted from the latter all that they wanted. . . .

A definite and decisive insurrection was not to be expected from these good people. There had been much disillusionment and much suffering; the most spirited of the young men were, for the most part—if they were not forced recruits in the Austrian army—in our own, in exile, or with me. Nevertheless, I was quite satisfied with the welcome they gave us, their eagerness in providing for our wants, and in giving us notice of the enemy's movements and furnishing us with guides where necessary; and especially with the care lavished on our wounded by the kindly Lombard women. The way we were received at Varese on the night following that of our crossing, is a thing very difficult to describe. It was raining heavily, yet I am sure that not a single citizen, man, woman, or child, was missing when we entered. It was a touching sight to behold. . . .

Urban was the Austrian general destined for our extermination. The first news I had of this ferocious enemy, coming from the direction of Brescia, was that he commanded 40,000 men. There were Austrians at Laveno, and another corps advancing from Milan—one might have been excused for shuddering at the situation.

The obligation we were under to defend Varese, and save it from the vengeance of Urban, who was said to be inexorable, caused me some apprehension. Had I been free to move in any direction outside the town, I should have had little fear of the enemy's numbers; but there was nothing very reassuring in being forced to await them at a fixed point in an unfortified town without a single gun, which could therefore make little or no preparation for serious resistance.

However, there was no help for it . . . [and the Austrians were defeated on May 25].

I knew the advantage to be gained by attacking an enemy thrown into confusion by a first defeat, however strong he may be, and did not wish to lose the opportunity of so doing. We left Varese, therefore, for Como, on the morning of May 27, by the Cavallasca road, reaching the latter village after midday. The men had done a great deal of marching, and were tired; but the hour was propitious. At nightfall one can attack even a superior force with comparatively little danger, especially in a mountainous position like that which was to be the scene of our enterprise, where the enemy's cavalry and artillery could be of little use.

I therefore let the men rest, and began to make all possible inquiries about the enemy's numbers, and the positions occupied by them; and, receiving intelligence that there were in force in the strong position of San Fermo (which I at once concluded to be the key to all the rest), I directed several companies, under the orders of the brave Captain Cenni, to turn this position on the right. Our second regiment was to attack in front, as soon as the flanking companies should have had time to reach the enemy's flank. The appointed time being over, Colonel Medici, with his usual gallantry, attacked the position in front, while Cenni, with the companies above mentioned, did so in flank.

The enemy bore up bravely against our attack, and fought with obstinate valor. The position was strong, commanding, and well fortified, so that the fight went on with the greatest fierceness for about an hour. At last, surrounded on all sides, the Austrians began to break and fly, and some of them surrendered. . . .

I have forgotten the names of many of my comrades who fell in that truly glorious action, in which a few raw and inexperienced lads scattered, with their impetuous onset, the far more numerous ranks of the ferocious Urban, who fled as far as Monza without turning back to see who had defeated him.

The possession of Como improved our situation by the acquisition of means of every kind—of credit, and of reinforcements in men and arms. The steamers, thanks to the good-will of the company and of their commanders, were ours, so that we were masters of the lake. All the villages of the lake, and the districts of Lecco and the Valtelline, had pronounced in our favor; everywhere men were asking for weapons to join in the patriotic enterprise.

THE ART OF IRREGULAR WARFARE [6]

Above all theory in the art of warfare, one practical fact reigns triumphant, *"defeat the enemy"*—a truth that will always

[6] Letter dated January 15, 1860, *The Court Journal,* London, January 28, 1860, p. 67.

triumph over all theories. The retreat of the most disciplined troops of Austria before the less disciplined Zouaves, proves that a man may be a soldier without wearing a tight tunic or a tight cravat. The shepherds of Paulus Emilius, armed only with daggers, rushing on the Macedonian phalanx, those terrible conquerors of Asia—the clouds of French Voltigeurs of the Army of the Republic—and, lastly, the Bersaglieri and Zouaves at St. Martino, Magenta, Solferino, and Palestro—prove that masses are not alone useful in battle-fields, and that Volunteers, Bersaglieri, and Zouaves, need not learn how to fight in close order, like troops of the line.

Discipline is, no doubt, the basis of the organization of all armaments, and without it war cannot be correctly carried on; but why should not volunteers, who have sworn not to abandon their standards during the danger of their country, have the same discipline as regular corps? Are patriotism and enthusiasm such despicable and heterogeneous sentiments as to destroy regularity in national troops? Certainly they are not despicable, since, in every war, a wise chief derives advantages from them in his harangues and his proclamations; and the First Napoleon, who was master of half Europe, and the best army in the world, was defeated by the patriotism of the English—so-called *shopkeepers*—of whom he appeared to have no great opinion. . . .

I believe that the theory of great regularity of masses and lines is generally carried too far, and that the open order of battle is too much neglected—as it has become necessary through the perfection of firearms, and through the obstacles that cultivation has accumulated at every step. If there is a country in Europe that has served for fields of battle, and continues to do so, that country is certainly, and unfortunately, Italy! How many places are there in Italy where a squadron formed in line, or a regiment in square, could fight? I believe that there are very few. On the other hand, places may be found in all directions which are adapted to the Bersaglieri [sharpshooters]. In short, I think that several lines of Bersaglieri, sustained by a few masses of troops, would be the most convenient order of battle in our country, and in many others; and that volunteers can be adapted, for this end, to the same kind of manoeuvres as the troops of the line.

I have read the valuable paper by Sir John Burgoyne on volunteers; and, although I do not know enough English, and have not had the time to form a thorough judgment upon it, it seems to me to be the work of an intelligent soldier, who has seen many fields of battle. I do not, however, agree with him that 50,000 veterans will defeat 100,000 volunteers, if the latter have the discipline that all troops ought to have; and that they are, as may be imagined, animated by the love of their country. I do not yet know the way in which the English volunteers are organized; but I believe, however, that for volunteers, in all countries, the training of the Bersaglieri is the best. The lightness of their uniform—the open order that forms the basis of their manoeuvring, without hindering them from acting in masses, when the occasion presents itself—and, above all, the swiftness of their movements—make them the most perfect soldiers I have known. I wish that all the Italian army was composed of Bersaglieri: and I do not doubt that such an organization would also be easily attainable by English volunteers—English soldiers having obtained the reputation of intrepidity and coolness under fire.

Honored by your question, I have replied to you as a friend to a friend—and such, also, should be all Italians with the noble and generous English nation.

4
The "Thousand" Capture Sicily

The year 1860 saw a complete breach between Gari-
baldi and the conservative Cavour. Throughout 1859, the
former had been entirely helpful and obedient: in Novem-
ber, for instance, to Mazzini's disgust, he had dutifully given
up his cherished plan to start a revolution in central Italy.
But early in 1860, an open clash was precipitated by the gov-
ernment's courageous yet provocative decision to give Savoy
and Nice (Garibaldi's birthplace) to France in return for
French permission to establish Piedmontese authority in
Tuscany.
   Another factor was that Garibaldi received secret encour-
agement to rebel from none other than the King himself. Vic-
tor Emanuel was anxious for a more adventurous policy than
his Prime Minister would countenance, and at one irresponsi-
ble moment told a friend that he would rather have Garibaldi
than Cavour as head of government (Giuseppe Massari,
Diario dalle cento voci, 1858–1860, ed. E. Morelli, Bologna,
1959, pp. 458, 463). It was especially pleasing to the King that
here was a man who would dare do anything, who could be
played off against the official ministers if necessary, yet who
could also be disavowed, in case of failure, without any risk
that he would give his sovereign away. As the Times *of Lon-*
don noted, this was a much more responsible Garibaldi than
the current myth allowed. He was not the melodramatic con-
spirator with broad sashes, vulgar pathos and verbal clap-
trap, but a man of loyalty and obedience, even something of a
statesman.

GARIBALDI SPEAKS AGAINST CAVOUR IN PARLIAMENT,
APRIL 12, 1860 [1]

Gentlemen. Article five of our Constitution says that "treat-
ies which involve altering the territory of the state shall have no

[1] *Atti del parlamento Italiano, sessione del 1860, Discussioni della Camera dei Deputati,* Turin, 1860, p. 84.

effect until parliament has approved them." Now this fundamental law means that any decrease in national territory, before this house has agreed to it, would be unconstitutional. That people in one province should be called upon to vote for joining another country—and that this should happen before this house has approved it, indeed before we have even decided whether such a vote should take place at all or what kind of vote it should be—this is a direct violation of the Constitution. . . .

In 1388 Nice joined itself to Piedmont on condition that it should never be alienated to any foreign power. But now the government, in the Treaty of March 24, has agreed to cede it to Louis Napoleon. Such action is also against natural law. If you reply that Nice has simply been exchanged for two more important provinces [Tuscany and the Romagna], it must still be said that any such traffic in peoples is repugnant to every civilized conscience. It would also set a dangerous precedent, and might undermine confidence in the future integrity of our country. ("Hear! Hear!")

The government justifies itself by citing the plebiscite which is due to take place on April 15 and 16—and in Savoy, with less haste, on the 22nd. But an enormous pressure is being brought to bear on the people of Nice, and this makes the vote thoroughly unfree. The presence of great numbers of policemen, the flatteries and threats which are continuously being employed, the direct pressure used by the government to force this union with France—a pressure you can observe in the proclamation issued by the governor Lubonis ("Bravo!" *from the galleries*)—the absence from Nice of many citizens for one reason or another, the precipitous haste in which this vote is being forced through, all these facts make it impossible to hold a truly free vote by universal suffrage.

THE DIARY OF FRANCESCO CRISPI, GENOA, MAY, 1860 [2]

Garibaldi's conquest of Sicily and Naples was the most remarkable military achievement by Italy in the whole risorgimento. What made it even more remarkable is that, when he first set out secretly from Genoa in two tiny paddle steamers, Garibaldi had only a thousand men with him, no ammunition, and only a few rusty, converted flintlock muskets that mostly would not fire. At the very outset, he had to

[2] *The Memoirs of Francesco Crispi*, ed. Thomas Palamenghi-Crispi, trans. Mary Prichard-Agnetti, London, 1912, Vol. I, 156–65.

evade, for five days at sea, the vigilance of both the Piedmon-
tese and Neapolitan navies, who both had orders to arrest
him, and he then had to fight a six month campaign against
the large, well-equipped army of the Neapolitan Bourbons.

May 5, 1860.

11 p.m.—Nino Bixio reads a proclamation from General Garibaldi, in which the names of the two steamers, *Piemonte* and *Lombardo,* are revealed (names that up to this moment had been kept
secret), belonging to the Genoese Steamship Company of Raffaele
Rubattino, which are to be taken possession of by force, if necessary. . . .

May 6

12:15 a.m.—The two steamers are boarded without opposition
from the sailors already on board, some of whom even consent to
reenlist on the same ship. The vessels lie at anchor side by side
at a pier near the dock. Those members of the crew who do not
wish to reenlist are permitted to go ashore.

While the *Piemonte* is preparing to start, the harbor-police
boat, on its rounds, comes to demand to what port the captain is
sailing; without giving any answer the commandant orders the
sailors to seize the boat that is lying alongside, and lash it to the
Piemonte. It is detained until the steamer is nearly ready to start,
when it is set free.

1:45 a.m.—The engines being ready on the *Piemonte,* but not yet
so on the *Lombardo* (which is the larger vessel), the *Piemonte* pre-
pares to tow her companion out of port. A wide détour is necessary
to avoid a French gun-boat anchored near the harbor mouth, from
which violence might be expected.

2:15 a.m.—General Garibaldi comes alongside in a small boat,
just outside the harbor. . . . The two steamers head for the beach
at Quarto, where the volunteers are assembled in small boats, each
having a lantern at the helm as a signal.

2:50 a.m.—Volunteers begin to come aboard both steamers on
the starboard side, while the coal and equipment prepared by Nino
Bixio are taken aboard on the port side. . . .

7:15 a.m.—The ammunition not having been delivered on
board the *Piemonte,* the General, supposing it to have been taken
aboard the *Lombardo,* gives the order to get under way. . . .

May 10

12:30 a.m.—General Garibaldi summons Castiglia to his deck cabin to consult him concerning a landing place. Castiglia fetches a chart of the Sicilian coast and spreads it before Garibaldi, who, following the southern coastline with a pair of compasses, pauses at Porto Palo near Menfi. This Porto Palo is but a narrow and very shallow bay, which only small craft may enter. . . .

These difficulties are explained to the General by Castiglia, who proposes Marsala as a more suitable spot. In the first place, it has a harbor which the steamers can enter, and moreover the disembarkation may be quickly accomplished by obtaining the use—either by force or persuasion—of boats belonging to ships in harbor, which are always numerous here. It is decided to land at Marsala, unless we find the enemy already there, in which case we shall disembark somewhere else on the southern coast of the island. . . .

May 11

12:45 p.m.—Our two steamers enter the harbor. The *Piemonte* casts anchor in the deepest part of the port, and brings her prow to windward. Bixio being ignorant of the bad state of the harbour, the *Lombardo* runs aground upon the bank of seaweed that for years has choked one side of the port, and remains with her stern turned in the opposite direction from the *Piemonte*'s prow, that is to say towards the E.S.E.

The disembarkation of the volunteers begins at once by means of the skiffs which all the ships anchored in the port—willingly or of necessity—have sent alongside the *Piemonte*. One English schooner freely offers her services.

THE DECISIVE VICTORY OF CALATAFIMI, IN A LETTER TO ROSOLINO PILO, MAY 16, 1860 [3]

Yesterday we fought and won. Our enemies fled in fear toward Palermo. The local population is very excited and is joining us wholesale. Tomorrow we march on Alcamo. Proclaim to Sicilians that now is the great moment to destroy the Bourbon regime, and we shall soon complete our victory. Any weapon will serve in the hand of a brave man—a musket, a scythe, an axe, or even a nail on the end of a stick. Join my forces and harass the enemy in any way possible. Try and have fires lit on all the hills round his forces.

[3] *Giuseppe Garibaldi, scritti politici e militari,* ed. Domenico Ciàmpoli, Rome, 1907, Vol. I, 149.

Shoot as much as possible at his sentries and advance posts by night. Cut his communications, and incommode him in every possible way.

AN ITALIAN NOVELIST, IPPOLITO NIEVO, DESCRIBES
THE CAPTURE OF PALERMO [4]

Just as I had feared, the Sicilian revolution proved to be non-existent. There were only some minor demonstrations in the towns and unrest among certain armed bands in the countryside, which were met by fierce reprisals by the Bourbon troops. That was all. It was on the rumor of a Sicilian revolution that we had risked death and drowning to arrive at Marsala, yet on arrival we found nothing. In northern Italy they took the news of Garibaldi's landing to mean that all was won and Sicily was free. We, on the contrary, having survived the dangers of the sea, still expected death on land either in battle or by execution. We pirates, as the Bourbons call us, could have hardly expected any better fate if caught.

This, no doubt, was why we gaily went ahead, thoughtlessly and without counting the cost. This was why we fought at Calatafimi with such desperate obstinacy that we began to be thought invincible. All credit to us for that! But the credit goes to Garibaldi for those two marches, first to Parco, then to Misilmeri, which made possible our sudden descent on Palermo. What a miracle! I swear to you, my darling Bice, that I can still hardly believe what I saw with my own eyes. The *picciotti*—the Sicilian word means young boys, and we use it for the armed bands because that is what they call themselves—simply ran away. And Palermo itself we found a city of the dead. There was no sign of any local rising until quite late in the day. We were on our own, eight hundred of us at most, spread out over an area as large as Milan.

It was impossible to expect any planning, let alone any orders, but somehow we managed to take the city against 25,000 regular soldiers. These well-armed and well-mounted troops of the enemy were just the sort of men [i.e., disciplined, well-armed regulars] who would delight the minister Lamarmora in Piedmont! We, on the other hand, were real ragamuffins. I myself was dressed just as when I left Milan, in trousers which exposed a good deal more than they should, and with a musket that fired only once in every four attempts. Yet to make up for this I had a loaf of bread spiked on my bayonet, and a fine cactus flower in my hat, with a splendid bedspread over my shoulders like a character from *Norma*. I must say I looked very pretty, and Garibaldi looked quite splendid. He was always seen in his shirt sleeves, and his only advantage over me was that his trousers instead of torn were decently patched. He entered Palermo with forty men; he then occupied the Piazza Bologna with thirty, and I think was almost alone apart from his son Menotti by the time he reached the city hall.

Meanwhile we all ran in ones and twos like sheep, through alleys and squares, chasing Neapolitans, and also to stir up the Palermitans to revolt or at least to make them build some barricades. But we succeeded only indifferently. For the Neapolitans were too busy running away and the Palermitans in seeking refuge from the indiscriminate gunfire which was now taking place. When Palermo finally fell, it had all been our doing, ours alone. Garibaldi showed the very height of courage, and we too were heroes just because we believed in what was strictly impossible. If these were not miracles, then St. Anthony is no saint.

DECREE OF THE DICTATOR OF SICILY, JUNE 13, 1860 [5]

Friedrich Engels, the communist leader who was at that time military correspondent for a New York paper, had already noted Garibaldi's preeminent military skill in the Lombard campaign of 1859. The manner in which the Bourbon generals were deluded and defeated in May, 1860 he now hailed as one of the most astonishing military enterprises of the century, the work of not a guerrilla leader but a general of real stature (The Daily Tribune, June 17, 1859, and June 22, 1860).

Some of Garibaldi's first decrees as Dictator of Sicily were measures of social reform dealing with land redistribution and popular education. Most of his energies, however, went to furthering the war, for he had every intention of keeping up the momentum through Sicily, up to Naples, and, if possible, to Rome and Venice too. He tried, without success, to introduce conscription. He organized a battalion of boys—not under 10 years old or over 17—who fought bravely, and most of whom were to be killed in the course of the campaign. A great deal of

[5] *Raccolta degli Atti del Governo Dittatoriale e Prodittatoriale in Sicilia, 1860,* Palermo, 1861, p. 49.

*time was also spent in foiling the efforts that Cavour was mak-
ing to undermine his authority and prevent his further advance.*

Garibaldi, in virtue of the powers conferred on him, and acting on the principle that a free people should change any of its customs which derive from a previous era of slavery, decrees:
Article 1. No one shall any longer address other people as "Your
Excellency."
Article 2. The *baciamano* [by which a serf would kiss the hand
of his landlord] is henceforth illegal.

Signed, G. Garibaldi, and F. Crispi.

CAVOUR'S ATTITUDE TO GARIBALDI: A LETTER TO
NIGRA IN FRANCE, AUGUST 1, 1860 [6]

If Garibaldi proceeds to the mainland of southern Italy and
captures Naples just as he has already taken Sicily and Palermo, he
will become absolute master of the situation. King Victor Emanuel
would lose almost all his prestige in the eyes of Italians, who would
look on him as little more than the friend of Garibaldi; and though
probably he would remain king, he would merely bask in such reflected glory as this heroic adventurer might decide to allow him.
Garibaldi, if he should reach Naples, would not proclaim a republic, but he would remain dictator, and would refuse to annex
southern Italy to Piedmont. His prestige would then be irresistible,
and, as he would dispose of the resources of a kingdom of nine million people, we could hardly cross him. He would be stronger than
we were. What then would remain to us? We would be forced to go
along with his plans and help him fight Austria. I am therefore convinced that the king must not receive the crown of Italy from
Garibaldi's hands, for his title to it would then be precarious, and
as a result we would be forced to take arms and try to win greater
prestige in Lombardy than Garibaldi has won in Sicily. Only the
capture of Verona and Venice would make people forget Palermo
and Milazzo.

[6] *Carteggi Cavouriani: Il carteggio Cavour-Nigra dal 1858 al 1861*, Bologna,
1929, Vol. IV, 122–24. Reprinted with the permission of the publishers, Nicola
Zanichelli, and the Ministero dell' Interno.

I have no illusions about the grave and dangerous decision I am advocating, but I believe it is essential if we are to save the monarchic principle. Better that a king of Piedmont should perish in war against Austria than be swamped by the revolution. The dynasty might recover from a defeat in battle, but if dragged through the revolutionary gutter its fate would be finally sealed.

Although I have made up my mind how to act if Garibaldi reaches Naples, it is nevertheless my first duty to the king and Italy to do everything possible to prevent his success there. My only hope of foiling him is if I can overthrow the Bourbon regime before Garibaldi crosses to the mainland—or at least before he has had time to reach Naples. If the regime falls, I would then take over the government of Naples in the name of order and humanity, and so snatch out of Garibaldi's hands the supreme direction of the Italian movement. This will need courage, audacity if you like; it will bring outraged protests from other countries, and may even force us sooner or later to fight against Austria. But it will save us from revolution. It will save the national and monarchic character of the Italian movement which is our glory and strength. . . .

A shipload of arms is therefore being sent to Naples for Liborio Romano to use there [Romano was a minister of the Bourbons whom Cavour had suborned]. Admiral Persano is also going to Naples on the pretext that the [Piedmontese] Princess of Syracuse has asked for our protection. Persano, Romano, and Nunziante [a Neapolitan general who had changed his allegiance] will arrange that a movement takes place among the citizens and in the Bourbon army and navy. If this succeeds, a provisional government will be established under Romano which will immediately invoke Piedmontese protection. Victor Emanuel will then accept a Protectorate, and troops will be landed to maintain order and stop Garibaldi's further advance.

GARIBALDI CRITICIZES CAVOUR FOR HINDERING THE "THOUSAND" IN 1860 [7]

Every possible obstacle was raised in our path [by Cavour and the Piedmontese government] between the time we left Genoa and when we arrived at Naples. Some people try to argue that the government could have stopped us and yet let us go, but I deny that

[7] Giuseppe Garibaldi, facsimile MSS., in *Il Risorgimento Italiano, rivista storica,* Turin, 1908, Vol. I, 12.

they could have stopped us. Public opinion was irresistibly on our
side from the first moment that news spread of the Sicilian rising in
April 1860. It is true that the government put no absolute veto in
our way [Garibaldi here wrote, and then crossed out, "hoping to be
rid forever of a lot of troublemakers like us"]; nevertheless they
raised every kind of obstacle. I was not allowed to take any of the
15,000 muskets which belonged to our Million Rifle Fund and were
kept by us in storage at Milan. This one fact delayed by several days
the sailing of our expedition. La Farina [a colleague of Cavour's]
then gave us just 1,000 bad firearms and 8,000 *lire*.

However, once we had taken Palermo, the liberation of all Sicily
became almost certain, and the Piedmontese government therefore
allowed a second expedition of volunteers to join us who proved of
great help. But Cavour's new plan was still that we should go no
further than Sicily, and with this purpose he sent La Farina and
others to campaign in Sicily for immediate annexation to Piedmont.
These men did all they possibly could to bring about their petty
objective [i.e. annexation, which would have prevented Garibaldi
going on to attack Naples]. . . .

Meanwhile hundreds of volunteers who were trying to join us
were prevented from doing so on one pretext or another, and even
arrested in order to keep them in northern Italy. My stocks of arms
at Parma were also confiscated. So urgent was our need of ammunition, that I sent to beg some from the Piedmontese naval ship stationed in Palermo harbor, but her commander abruptly refused
and called my messenger a spy.

Even greater difficulties were placed in my path at Naples. Everyone knows how Cavour sent a host of secret agents there who did
what they could with the local conservative committee to bring
about their own revolution before I had time to reach Naples. It
is also common knowledge that, just when I was preparing to fight
the battle on the river Volturno, I was forced to leave the army and
go back to Sicily in order to calm the agitation there which had
been brought about by other agents sent from Turin.

GARIBALDI TO DEPRETIS, SEPTEMBER 9, 1860 [8]

I was on the point of agreeing to your request to proclaim the
annexation of Sicily to the other liberated provinces. But, for the

[8] Ida Nazari-Micheli, *Cavour e Garibaldi nel 1860, cronistoria documentata*,
Rome, 1911, p. 159.

moment, I have decided to deny myself this pleasure, because I am absolutely sure that annexation, or to put it properly the proclamation of a united Italy under Victor Emanuel as king, should be effected only when the Italian people have fought their way all the way from Sicily as far as Rome. For Rome is the capital of Italy. You can surely understand that immediate annexation might signify rather the detachment of one province from its revolutionary solidarity with those not yet conquered. The revolution has proved to be our salvation; and hence annexation, by ending the revolution, might mark the end of everything.

5

Garibaldi Gives Southern Italy to King Victor Emanuel

Cavour failed to stop Garibaldi reaching Sicily, and then failed to prevent him crossing the Straits of Messina to the mainland of southern Italy; but the nearer this volunteer army came to Rome, the greater danger there was of running into armed opposition from the French. The Piedmontese government therefore tried to annex Sicily by instigating a pronunciamento *in Palermo against Garibaldi's authority. At the same time, while pretending to remain on friendly terms with the Neapolitan government, Cavour secretly poured money and arms into Naples, hoping to provoke internal defections and to capture the city from the Bourbons before these dangerous firebrands could arrive there.*

Garibaldi knew how to make revolutions, and the conservatives did not, with the result that Cavour was forced to acknowledge defeat, and did so gracefully. He admitted that the conquest of southern Italy was "the most poetic fact of the century," and that Garibaldi had been far more successful than himself in attracting support all over Europe for the cause of Italian nationality: what is more, "he has given the Italians self-confidence; he has proved to Europe that Italians can fight and die to reconquer their fatherland." (Il carteggio Cavour-Nigra, *Bologna, 1929, Vol. IV, 149*).

Most remarkable of all, perhaps, Garibaldi was ready to stand down unostentatiously at his moment of greatest power, and, after six months of dictatorial rule, handed Sicily and Naples to the government of Piedmont. He insisted on correcting a Swiss journalist who said that he had "conquered" these provinces, for he had merely helped them to deliver themselves (S. F. Baridon, Marc-Monnier e l'Italia, *Turin, 1942, p. 229). He himself was too busy to write much at the time, so the course of these events is here told by others.*

THE CAPTURE OF NAPLES [1]

Pushing our way through a crowd of monks, priests, and peasants, we were ushered into a small room upstairs, where on one side was a knot of Garibaldi's most intimate officers already engaged in washing off the dust which lay almost an inch thick on their faces, while on the other side, in front of the garret window, standing before a broken mirror, was Garibaldi himself in red shirt and grey trousers with belt, a Calabrian hat under his arm, while his hands were occupied in combing his long hair with a slow, meditative movement. He seemed not to pay the slightest attention to the babel of sounds around him, and we stood by him for full five minutes without his being aware of our presence. When he at last turned and saw us he smiled, shook hands, and made us sit down. He then began to talk in a strange mixture of French and English, although all the while he never ceased to comb his hair. We told him how we had come from England to witness his entry into Naples; we told him of the sympathy England had for him; and, what was more practical, we gave him all the information we had picked up in Naples about the movements of the troops and of the King, etc. We mentioned to him the French designs upon Naples, and he said that he was quite aware of them. . . .

Garibaldi further informed us that he had no objection whatever to our joining the staff that followed him, provided we donned and continued to wear red shirts. He added that in view of the varied and doubtful character of the many hangers-on to his small army, the only safety from robbery for strangers like us lay in the adoption of this characteristic dress. Thus launched on our short career as Garibaldians, we quickly rubbed acquaintance with some of the others—a motley, but interesting lot. There were Türr and Eber, both Hungarians; Dunne and Dowling, Englishmen, with Frank Vizetelly as newspaper correspondent: there were Cosenz, Stagnetti, and Gusmaroli, Italians; and, as a foil to all these rough men, a beautiful Contessa de la Torre, dressed like a Hussar, but with a neat skirt of brown holland. She had come up with the Garibaldians all the way from Palermo, and had acted mainly as *vivandière* to the regiment. Her enthusiasm for her cause and country, combined with youth and a slight figure, made her a very attractive

[1] *The National and English Review*, London, 1899, Vol. XXXIII, 495–97, "A Garibaldi reminiscence," by Evelyn Ashley, secretary to Lord Palmerston.

personality. But we had not time for much palaver, as an entry into Salerno was ordered for next day. The Neapolitan troops had evacuated it the previous night—that is to say, 5,000 Bavarians had retreated before 500 Calabrians and the magic of Garibaldi's name —a judicious use of the telegraph wires having greatly contributed to this result by magnifying the number and multiplying the positions of his troops, the main body of whom were, in fact, still sixty or seventy miles behind. It was really a comedy, and could only be accounted for by the complete demoralization of the hired foreigners who acted (so ineffectually) as King Ferdinand's bulwarks. . . .

The next day, the 7th September, 1860, is one that ought never to fade from the calendar of Naples or be obliterated from the memory of its inhabitants. It witnessed an event absolutely unique in history. A capital city occupied and its government assumed by a mere handful of men, who brought with them hope and liberty, and drove out despotism and despair—the former ruler having only taken his departure a few hours previously, and having left many thousands of his troops still in the two citadels, with directions that those in St. Elmo should bombard the town as soon as the Liberator arrived.

But to return. A deputation of the National Guard arrived from Naples during the night, as well as an energetic appeal from the Revolutionary Committee; so Garibaldi determined to enter the capital—and by train! He was evidently intensely glad and relieved at having received information that there would be no armed resistance, both from his sincere desire to avoid effusion of blood and also from his wish, as he said, to show to Europe that he was entering not by force, but by the will and amid the acclamations of the people. This was true even of the *Lazzaroni,* who, comprising the most ignorant and violent of the population, had hitherto been the slavish adherents of absolutism. But they had been won over by the efforts of Liborio Romano, who, though one of Ferdinand's Ministers, had been preparing the ground for the advent of liberty. A special train was got ready to carry Garibaldi from La Cava, about three miles north of Salerno, to Naples. It started at nine in the morning. We got places in it. It consisted only of four carriages. Thirteen of his staff besides ourselves formed his only companions. The roofs, as well as all the spare seats, were crowded with National Guards. We slowly crept along, finding that the large populations of Torre del Greco, Resina, and Portici had taken complete possession of the line, so that we had to make frequent halts to avoid running over this shouting mass of men, women, and children.

A FOREIGN VOLUNTEER AT THE BATTLE OF
THE VOLTURNO, APRIL 1, 1860 [2]

Garibaldi, while intending to keep the defensive, was perfectly ready to take the offensive at the first opportunity.

At six o'clock, 16,000 [of the enemy] had left Capua; 5,000 of these were cavalry. At the same time 5,000 men marched on to Maddaloni to cut off the retreat of the Garibaldians by taking them in the rear. As soon as Egerton and myself heard the firing, we rushed off up the street, where we were met by an old man, who said the Neapolitans had driven the Garibaldians over the fifteen arches of the railway, and that he apprehended the worst. Thinking, right or not, that St. Angelo would give us the best chance of service, Egerton and I, in spite of the balls and grape-shot now hotly whistling about on every side, started off for St. Angelo, along the dusty high road from Santa Maria.

That morning, profiting by the thick mists which rise from the low ground near the river, I had seen them so thick indeed—and they were at that time—that you could hardly see with any certainty at the least distance—[the enemy] had advanced nearly up to a barricade constructed to guard a position at a point where a by-road from Capua to St. Angelo cuts the road from Santa Maria, where the road turns up to St. Angelo.

They had affected this advance under cover of the dry beds of mountain torrents, steep and well screened with brushwood. With the nature of the ground, and the thick white mist likewise in their favor, they rushed at the barricade with terrible impetuosity, and drove the Garibaldini at first across the main road, right away towards St. Angelo. Along the road are open fields, where I have many a time since then sat and boiled my coffee in my canteen over a wood fire, or with writing-case on my knee indited letters to my friends at home, with the scene vividly before me. Taking up position there, they formed well.

They had, it seems, been equally successful on the left; for they had driven the Garibaldians also away from a trench near the river.

[2] W. B. Brooke, *Out with Garibaldi; or From Milazzo to Capua*, London, 1860, pp. 136–39.

Moreover, a column of theirs had actually got up a hill which commands St. Angelo.

Nothing but the genius of Garibaldi in that terrible hour could have turned his fortunes so far. He arrived in the very nick of time. He came along rapidly with his staff in carriages from Santa Maria, and was rattling along the main road with grape-shot and bullets flying over him. Very soon was he in sight of the enemy, when luckily the carriages, except one, had time to turn into a covered way. The last carriage was smashed by a cannon-ball.

On through the covered way then went the General with his "six-shooter" in his hand towards St. Angelo. When he arrived his men gave a shout. His presence now as ever was their best stimulant.

The enemy had a column in the rear on the hills to the left. But some skirmishers were thrown out on the heights above them. Then on came thundering the Neapolitan cavalry; but this time they met no cravens. The fierce Calabrese emptied their saddles, bayonetted them, and in one or two instances slew them with their stilettoes. And yet, glorious as it is to see brave men in a good cause dying for freedom with Spartan fortitude, it seemed to me something like a desecration of the loveliness of the scene, on which the sun shone brightly, all this carnage and fearful slaughter. What struck me at the time more than anything else, was the stern, silent determination with which every man fought. This time there were no rallying cries, no encouraging shouts—not a word—but grim, deadly conflict. Foemen standing before foemen with bent brows and compressed lips in stern hate, asking no quarter and giving none.

Then a red cloud came before my eyes, and I seemed to feel no more, save that I was one in a *melée,* shooting away, or bayonetting, or using a revolver as opportunity offered. And the calm sun all this while, and the green olive trees looked down on us at our work of death, as so many stern and silent foemen drove their reeking bayonets into the hearts of their adversaries, and riflemen sent their deadly bullets crashing through some hussar's brain. Then were steeds screaming harshly in their agony, and running riderless among us. Then were seen fierce death-struggles in several places, Calabrese locked in conflict with Neapolitans till the pistol or the dagger settled the matter. There were not really, though nominally three brigades besides the Calabrese and Genoese, more than 3,000 men there of ours that day. The Neapolitans had actually three times that number.

Our main object was to take care of the main road to Santa Maria and the pontoons, etc., prepared towards the river. Bloody work it was for all. We had to push our line of defense further than the actual main road itself, and come down well into the open. As for defensive works, we there had none, save a barricade of sandbags with four guns on the road leading from Capua to St. Angelo. All day long there was terrific fighting going on for the possession of the barricade. I saw John Egerton that day doing his duty like an Englishman who is in earnest. What better description can I give than that to Englishmen? I saw Garibaldi, with his red shirt wringing wet with perspiration, his eye sternly gleaming, his face flushed with the heat of conflict, and blackened by the smoke and dust. I heard his voice commanding—but it was no longer now the calm, clear voice of quieter times. It was hoarse and guttural, and choked with emotion. For the good general saw his gallant band unfalteringly pouring out their life-blood.

ALBERTO MARIO WATCHES GARIBALDI MEET THE KING, OCTOBER 26, 1860 [3]

Garibaldi did not tarry long, and dismounting, he stood gazing with evident satisfaction on the [royalist] troops. The [royalist] General Della Rocca advanced courteously. A few officers greeted [Garibaldi] with beaming faces; but the greater part passed on with the prescribed salute, unconscious of, or indifferent to the presence of the Liberator of the Two Sicilies. Indeed an impartial observer of the respective physiognomies would have taken them for the liberators and him for the liberated. Presently the drums beat, and the musicians struck up the royal march.

"It is the King," said General Della Rocca. "The King! the King!" burst from every lip. A group of carabineers on horse, forming the bodyguard, armed with swords, handcuffs, and thumbscrews [Mario was a republican and a follower of Mazzini!], announced the presence of the Sardinian monarch. The King, in general's uniform, rode a piebald Arab, and behind him came a long train of generals, chamberlains, and orderlies: Fanti, the Minister of War, and Farini, viceroy of Naples *in pectore,* who was wrapped in and embarrassed by a large military tunic. All were alike adverse to Garibaldi—to this plebeian donor of a realm. The

[3] Alberto Mario [aide to Garibaldi], *The Red Shirt: Episodes,* London, 1865, pp. 284–88.

Dictator's appearance was singular that morning. Under his little pork-pie hat he had tied his foulard, to protect his ears from the morning dew—so that when he lifted his hat to the King the handkerchief remained knotted under his chin. The King held out his hand, saying, "Ah! hello my dear Garibaldi; how are you?"

"Well, your Majesty; and you?"

"Fine!"

Raising his voice, and turning to the crowd, the Dictator cried, "Hail to the King of Italy!"; and all responded, *"Viva il Re!"*

Moving on one side to allow the troops to pass, the King and the Dictator chatted together for a few minutes. I happened to be close to them, and I confess that I was curious to hear for the first time in my life a king's discourse—to judge for myself whether lofty sentiments would correspond with the grandeur of the situation. Campanian soil—Capua at hand—shades of Hannibal and Roman consuls—the meeting of the armies of Castelfidardo and Maddaloni —the eve of battle—presence of the conquering prince and of the man of the people, donor of a realm—contact of the red shirt and royal purple—transformation of a petty king into the King of Italy —all combined to render the situation truly epic.

The King talked of the fine weather and of the bad roads, interrupting the conversation to administer gruff reproofs and manual checks to his fiery and restless steed; then they rode on, Garibaldi at the King's left, and, a few paces behind, the Sardinian and Garibaldian staff pell-mell; but soon each returned to his own center— in one line the modest redshirts, in the other the splendid uniforms shining with gold, silver, crosses, medals, and the *gran cordone*. But in the midst of a pervading sensation of the vanity of human grandeur, arose the consoling thought of the sumptuous breakfast which the royal cooks had gone to prepare at Teano.

Meanwhile the clash of arms, the shining plumes and helmets, had attracted all the peasants of the environs, who hailed Garibaldi with their usual enthusiasm. He was at his wits' end to direct their attention from himself to the King, and keeping his horse a few paces behind, he cried, with an imperious gesture, "This is Vittorio Emanuele, the King, your King, the King of Italy. *Viva il Re!*" The peasants stared and listened: then, not understanding the tenor of his speech, again shouted, *"Viva Galibardo!"* The poor General was on the rack, and knowing how dear to princes is applause, and how much his popularity irritated the King, would have given a second kingdom to wring from the lips of those unsophisticated boors an *evviva* to the King of Italy, who ended the question by spurring his horse into a gallop. We of course galloped after him; and even Farini, grasping his saddle, careless of reins or stirrups, galloped too, his trowsers working gradually upwards until his knees were left bare. Fortunately for him, the King reined in his horse as soon as the boors were passed, and the future viceroy had time to adjust his trowsers, smooth down his tunic, set his hat straight, and wipe the perspiration from his brow.

Arrived at the bridge which crosses the little stream near Teano, I saw Garibaldi lift his hat to the King, and take the road leading across country, while his Majesty crossed the bridge. Thus they parted at right angles, the royalists following the King, we Garibaldi. He dismounted at a little village, and led his horse into an outhouse on the road. Missori, Nullo, Zasio, and myself posted our horses on an adjacent mound, and looked at each other in blank amazement. Entering the outhouse, I found the General standing by a barrel, on which his orderly had laid the breakfast, i.e., a piece of bread and cheese and a glass of water, which, as soon as he had drunk, he spat out, saying, "There must be a dead animal at the bottom of the well." Slowly and silently we retraced our steps to Calvi, near the Volturno. Garibaldi's countenance was full of melancholy sweetness; never did I feel drawn to him with such tenderness.

A FRENCHMAN AT NAPLES WATCHES GARIBALDI HAND OVER TO THE KING [4]

On November 5 all the Garibaldian troops still stationed in Naples received orders to move out to Caserta where the King had agreed to accord them an official review. There they waited all day long on the 6th, but in vain, for Victor Emanuel, presumably so as not to annoy the regular troops of his own northern army, did not deign to appear before our "volunteer bands." There was also another explanation of this episode, because all the volunteers of the southern army were as a result away at Caserta on the 7th when the King was due to make his solemn entry into Naples.

There were thus only one or two red-shirted officers watching as spectators on a balcony as the King entered Naples. It was the Piedmontese troops and the Neapolitan national guard who lined the

[4] Maxime Du Camp, *Expédition des Deux-Siciles: souvenirs personnels,* Paris, 1861, pp. 349–51.

road, and of Garibaldians there was no sign. Yet it had been these Garibaldians who had conquered Sicily, who had delivered Calabria and dispersed the Bourbon army, who had taken Naples and then splendidly resisted an attack before Capua, and finally, by themselves, won the battle of the Volturno. It seemed only natural that they should be sent away on the day of their triumph!

The weather was terrible and did no honor to Italy. It rained in torrents. A fierce west wind blew in continual gusts. In the harbor the swell tossed the ships until their lower yards were awash. Everything was sad and cold. One might say that an evil fairy—that of gratitude perhaps had waved her wand over the preparations for this ceremony. None of the preparations had in fact been completed. Stretched over the wet roads were decorative figures still without heads; and their hands, which were intended to hold flags, were empty. Colored bunting, after being torn by the wind and soaked by the storm, flapped against the bare scaffolding. Triumphal arches were a mere shell and nothing but bare boards. The whole thing was pitiful.

An immense crowd filled the streets all the way from the railway station to the royal palace, but all you could see was umbrellas. From above and from far away they looked like an army of giant mushrooms. At 10 o'clock the guns of the forts thundered out and the King rode to the cathedral accompanied by Garibaldi. The latter, as soon as he arrived there, was set upon by the women and embraced far more than he must have liked. Thence Victor Emanuel travelled by carriage past the shouts and petitions of the crowd to the palace. On his left sat Garibaldi in his grey cloak. In front of the King, and wearing a dark suit, was the pro-dictator of Naples, Pallavicino, and Antonio Mordini the pro-dictator of Sicily in a red shirt. Mordini had done wonderful things in Sicily, and everyone was glad that he sat in the royal carriage in the dress which above all should have been seen on this day. The red shirt in fact symbolizes the revolution which has won Italian independence, and it was this red shirt which should have done the honors to Victor Emanuel at Naples; nor, I think, could the King have objected to that. Pallavicino was now given the grand cordon of the Order of Santa Annunziata, but Garibaldi and Mordini refused it. [The correct story was that the King did not offer it to the red-shirted Mordini, as a deliberate sign of his royal displeasure.]

Is it true that Garibaldi asked Victor Emanuel to let him govern Italy for one year with dictatorial powers? I think so, but cannot be certain for I did not personally hear the request made. It is too much in character for one not to believe it. Garibaldi's idea apparently is to introduce compulsory military service for the whole country and to attack the Austrians in Venice next spring with such force that resistance would be hopeless. The King refused, retreating behind the Piedmontese constitution which reserves all such exceptional measures for the decision of parliament.

Two days later, on November 9, just before dawn, Garibaldi rowed himself in a small dinghy to a steamboat placed at his disposal to take him home to Caprera. Of all his army, he took with him only his old faithful friends, Basso and Froscianti. Of the enormous sums which had passed through his hands, he had no more than 10 piastres, a mere 50 francs. This was a day of silence for the Garibaldians at Naples. We were all sad, and all knew that something fine had gone out of our lives. That evening, however, an immense procession moved through the town to the cry of "Long live Garibaldi!"

6
In Opposition to the Italian Government

Cavour wanted to seem not too ungrateful for Garibaldi's peaceful cession to him of Naples and Sicily, but at the same time he felt he should use this welcome turn of events in order to defeat all that the revolutionaries stood for; and, hence, in his choice of officials to take over from them, he was brave enough (or ill-advised enough) to select only Garibaldi's personal enemies. Apart from Fanti, the military commander, the man Cavour appointed as Governor of Naples, Luigi Carlo Farini, refused to shake hands with, or even to speak to, the radical leader, on those occasions at Naples when they had to meet; and, to strengthen his self-confidence, Farini was empowered by Cavour to "exterminate" the Garibaldians and drive them into the sea if they did not submit (Carteggi di Camillo Cavour: La Liberazione del Mezzogiorno, *Bologna, 1952, Vol. III, 64, 326*).

Garibaldi, at this period of his greatest triumph, had enough self-control to swallow a succession of deliberate insults, and used all his prestige to make southerners accept Victor Emanuel's government with enthusiasm. In return, the King gratefully agreed to grant his main request—that his volunteers and those who had served as ministers in his dictatorial government should be treated well.

When the news of this single concession reached Turin, however, Cavour threatened resignation and forced the King to back down. Among Garibaldi's ministers were the two most famous Italian Prime Ministers of the next half century; these men and their colleagues received no thanks but a good deal of sarcastic disparagement for what they had done, and only some 1,700 of the now 50,000-strong army of volunteers were taken into the regular army (Luigi Mondini, "L'unificazione delle forze armate," Atti del XL Congresso di Storia del

Risorgimento Italiano, *Turin, 1961, p. 332). When the ex-dictator finally left Naples for Caprera, the Piedmontese fleet had orders not to take the least notice of his departure, and only foreign naval ships in the bay fired their guns. It may be that Cavour did not think this could be construed as ingratitude, but some of his own party were soon wondering whether such treatment of Garibaldi might not prove, at all events, somewhat impolitic.*

KING VICTOR EMANUEL TO CAVOUR, FROM NAPLES, NOVEMBER 22, 1860 [1]

You will have seen that I quickly put an end to that very disagreeable question of what to do with Garibaldi. He is neither as docile nor as honest as people say and as you yourself think. He has very little military talent, as his failure to take Capua proves, and he has done enormous damage at Naples. For example there has been a barefaced theft of all the money collected in taxes, and this must be blamed on him and the rabble who surround him. They have plunged this unhappy country into a quite frightening state.

I wish I could say that the question of his army could be easily solved. I myself knew exactly what had to be done, and felt strong enough to do it, and certainly had more ability to do it than anyone else. But General Fanti, who is a fine fellow in his own way, but of whom I have had many reasons to complain during this campaign, did absolutely nothing to preserve even the ordinary forms of civility. So doing, he annoyed everyone, and if I and most of Garibaldi's generals had not intervened, there would have been an armed revolution and blood would have flowed.

The volunteers, who rightly or wrongly think they have done a good job, have in the end been treated like dogs. Fanti behaves toward them in public with a sovereign contempt, and I have seen him ill-use even those of them who have been crippled with wounds and are asking for alms. But there is too much to write, and too much to tell you. I will only say that it has caused me immense pain. We have thus been put firmly in the wrong. At Turin it was not

[1] "Vittorio Emanuele, Cavour e Garibaldi, cinque lettere inedite," ed. Luigi Mondini, *Nuova Antologia di Scienze, Lettere ed Arti*, Rome, August, 1960, Vol. CDLXXIX, 497–98. Reprinted with permission of the Deputazione Subalpina di Storia Patria.

possible to see things as I can see them here, and if only you had been here and observed the volunteer ranks as I have, if you had seen their gaiety and their wonderful spirit when fighting, if you had like myself seen 1,800 of their wounded men at Naples and Caserta (without counting those in Sicily), perhaps you would have thought as I did, and perhaps you would have praised the courage of these unfortunate volunteers—a courage which Fanti has poured ridicule on in public. The treatment they should have been given was known by everyone, even by the volunteers themselves, and they were ready to accept it; but at least one should have taken trouble to see that the honor of this corps received proper consideration.

We have now reached the position where Garibaldi's generals and Fanti cannot get on with each other at all. The dissolution of Garibaldi's volunteers is bringing with it a great hatred, and this has done grave damage and may yet do more. I am sorry to say all this, but I write just as thoughts come to me, and in this case I know I am not wrong.

GARIBALDI IN PARLIAMENT, APRIL 18, 1861 AS SEEN BY A FRENCH DIPLOMAT IN TURIN [2]

The session opened at 1:30 p.m. as usual. All the ministers were in their places. Toward 2 o'clock the shouting of the crowd outside reached the deputies and warned them that Garibaldi had arrived. As he entered, suddenly there was tremendous applause in the galleries of parliament. A small door opened high up behind the benches on the left. Garibaldi walked in, wearing his usual dress, his immortal red shirt with a grey overmantle like a chasuble or a Mexican poncho. It all made him look like a prophet—or, if you prefer, like an old vaudeville actor. All the deputies except about fifteen on the left remained in their seats and waited patiently for four or five minutes until the din subsided.

The cold silence of parliament made a singular contrast with the applause from the galleries, and indeed it was noticeable that there were no citizens of Turin among these applauding visitors. Garibaldi, with the two deputies who accompanied him, took his seat on the extreme left, and the session resumed. The new deputy was administered the oath by the Speaker. Baron Ricasoli then finished

[2] Henry D'Ideville, *Journal d'un Diplomate en Italie, 1859–1862,* Paris, 1872, Vol. I, pp. 179–88.

his interpellation about the volunteers in Garibaldi's army, and the minister of war, General Fanti, read a long written reply, very firm and very energetic on the subject of the Garibaldians.

At this point, amid profound silence, Garibaldi rose. Everybody waited with profound emotion, knowing how important would be his words in view of the present party tensions. Everyone knew perfectly well how Garibaldi hated Cavour's cabinet, as everyone also knew the open antagonism between Garibaldi's volunteers and the regular army, and all this gave an added interest to the debate.

One must not forget the position held by Garibaldi in Italy at this moment. Conqueror of the kingdom of the two Sicilies, acclaimed by five millions of Italians as their liberator, generalissimo of an army which he had himself created, surrounded by the prestige of victory and an enormous popularity, he had won for himself an extraordinary position, and the flatterers around him had had every interest in increasing it still further. His boundless pride had been overexcited by ovations from the downtrodden citizens of Naples. Arrogant toward the government, insolent to parliament, he spared the deputies no insults. He had even dared to treat the king with familiarity as an equal. But Turin was strongly monarchical, and among her citizens Garibaldi was very unpopular, even thought to be dangerous. . . .

His speech started badly. The Left, in other words the Garibaldians, were pained by the deplorable effect he was having, when suddenly, abandoning the parliamentary forms which he obviously found such a burden, Garibaldi irritably pushed aside his notes which strewed the table and began to extemporize. At once the scene changed. From being ridiculous and painful, it became tragic. With menacing voice and gesture, he turned to the ministerial bench and declared "that he could never shake hands with a man [Cavour] who had sold Nice to a foreign power, nor could he support a government which had clumsily tried to stir up civil war."

At these words the whole chamber was on its feet, while the galleries broke into cheers. Cavour, leaning on the table with his eyes fixed on Garibaldi, until now had kept his temper despite these accusations. He rose, pale and trembling, to protest against such terrible imputations. Everyone was crying "Order! Order! It is disgraceful!"

A veritable tumult then took place, made worse by the applause and the din up in the galleries. Deputies rushed from their seats toward the ministerial benches. A representative of the Left was seen to threaten Cavour with his fist. While others seized this man to take him away, Cavour himself was replying with vigor. Angry groups were in violent debate everywhere. Every kind of insult and rebuke was being hurled to and fro, though the noise and the disorder prevented most of them reaching their mark. Shouts and threats were even heard coming from the ambassadorial gallery, and frightened ladies were trying to escape from a dramatic and tumultuous scene which recalled the worst days of the French Convention. . . .

Many sensible and passionately patriotic Italians still found it hard to believe that their idol, their hero, was no more than this poor simpleton, brave and disinterested no doubt, but with a limitless pride which has destroyed even his common sense. Nevertheless, as he left parliament, Garibaldi was accompanied to his home by the same cheering crowds of his partisans who had filled the parliamentary galleries.

Garibaldi was soon engaged in prodding the government to plan another war, so that Italy could acquire Rome and Venice. In the Spring of 1862, he was summoned from Caprera to see the King and the new Prime Minister, Urbano Rattazzi. He was also given a substantial secret subsidy by the government. Whatever the nature of their bargain, Garibaldi immediately acted as though authorized to start another movement like that which had conquered the South in 1860, and Rattazzi did nothing to stop him from organizing and arming a private force of some 4,000 men, with the unconcealed program of "Rome or death."

The only plausible explanation of this episode is that the government was in collusion with Garibaldi, hoping that this force would quickly reach the Papal States and so give the Italian army an excuse to occupy Rome and "restore order." As the volunteers marched through Sicily, any overly inquisitive officials were effectively silenced by being shown a mysterious piece of paper. For nearly a week, the Garibaldians then occupied Catania, one of the larger towns in Italy, and no one interfered with them or stopped them when they took over several ships and embarked for the mainland. Pius IX was sufficiently alarmed to think of abandoning his kingdom, and made enquiries whether he would be allowed to live in England without being bothered by "those violent protestants whose speeches he read in the newspapers" (The Roman Question, ed. Blakiston, op. cit., p. 235).

As soon as Rattazzi and his colleagues realized that their own connivance in this escapade was public knowledge, they changed direction abruptly. Garibaldi was outlawed like a brigand or a rebel, just for trying to do once again what he had been so applauded for doing in 1860. He was then seriously wounded in an engagement with the Italian army at Aspromonte in Calabria during which some on both sides were killed. The soldiers did not even call upon him to surrender before opening fire. Many medals for bravery were given to the army after this pitiful skirmish, although the Garibaldians had had orders not even to load their rifles, and some of them had been prominently displaying a white flag.

Aspromonte gave the French Stock Exchange its best day for two years, but it was the most terrible moment in Garibaldi's life. Some of his men who surrendered were at once executed without trial, as deserters from the regular army—despite factual doubts about this accusation, and despite the fact that deserters who had joined the "Thousand" in 1860 had earned promotion rather than execution (Pagine Rare di Storia Garibaldina, ed. Oreste Mandalari, Rome, 1933, pp. 71–75). *Garibaldi reacted with extreme bitterness, and decided to publish a book in England which would explain the King's involvement; but then changed his mind when he saw that this might gravely damage the nation* (Jessie White Mario, In memoria di Giovanni Nicotera, *Florence, 1894, pp. 60–61). As it was thought too dangerous to punish him or even bring him to trial, he was then "pardoned" and set free.*

A SHORT ADDRESS TO THE STUDENTS OF PARMA, MARCH 30, 1862 [3]

Some of us have already passed our peak; but you, on the other hand, you students stand for the Italy of the future, and our hopes are firmly on you. Freedom can be won only if you learn how to fight for it. I do not say that you should give up your studies to take part in military training. Study and knowledge edify the mind. Yet our main need is now for soldiers. Some of our Italian provinces are still enslaved, and it is no good blaming this fact on others or on the government, for the fault is in large part our own.

The time will come when the states of Europe can afford to think more of humanity at large. Then there will be no more standing

[3] *Il Diritto,* April 2, 1862, in *Edizione Nazionale degli Scritti di Giuseppe Garibaldi,* Bologna, 1935, Vol. V, 47.

armies or fleets. When that happens, the great expenditure now
devoted to destroying oppressors (or in oppressing others) will be
used instead to help the poorer classes.

ADDRESS GIVEN IN A CHURCH AT COMO, MAY 27, 1862, TO COMMEMORATE THOSE KILLED IN BATTLE [4]

Man's life, like that of the flowers of the field, is not judged
just by its length. Nor does it matter much if we live one day more
or less. By our fruits we shall be judged. Those whose deaths we
celebrate here did not die in vain, and their death will be the seed
of new life.

I envy them. (*The crowd sighed.*) Yes, I envy them, for they at
least have done their duty, and their memory will be blessed for
ever more. But the rest of us must stay alive. There is still much to
hope for. There is, for example, ("Rome and Venice," *shouted a
thousand voices, interrupting him*).

Yes, Rome and Venice. (*Here the speaker clenched his fists on
his cap as emotion overcame him.*) There is much more left for us
to do. It is a shame, a crying shame. (*Here he stopped speaking,
being so moved that words failed him, and the crowd understood
and wept.*)

RATTAZZI'S GOVERNMENT TURNS AGAINST GARIBALDI, AUGUST 20, 1862 [5]

Your Majesty, we have to report to you that General Garibaldi, forgetting his duty as a subject, has raised the banner of rebellion in Sicily. He is trying to deceive simple people by claiming
to act in your name and that of Italy, but this is merely to conceal
the secret plans of those international revolutionaries in Europe in
whose service he now seems to have enlisted his sword and his
fame. . . .

Deaf to the voice of duty, he has no scruples at all over igniting
a civil war inside his own country. Your own influence with him,
which was once so great, is without effect. Something more energetic
is now needed. . . .

[4] *Il Diritto,* May 30, 1862, in *Edizione Nazionale degli Scritti di Giuseppe Garibaldi,* Vol. V, 84.
[5] Luigi Zini, *Storia d'Italia dal 1850 al 1866,* Milan, 1869, Vol. II, part II,
796–98.

Now that rebellion is open, the ministers composing your government would be unworthy of your confidence and that recently granted us by parliament if we did not put to you our proposal, namely that every means which law and natural reason allow to your royal authority should be employed, so that this bold revolt should be repressed wherever it has shown itself, and the rule of law be restored throughout Sicily. . . .

By raising his own flag against yours, and arming ordinary citizens against your loyal troops, General Garibaldi has made himself an outlaw. He and his followers are in open hostility against the state, and so we must treat those areas of the country which they occupy as though held by a national enemy. [Signed by Rattazzi, Depretis, and all the other ministers]

DR. ALBANESE RECOUNTS GARIBALDI'S ENGAGEMENT WITH THE ITALIAN ARMY AT ASPROMONTE, AUGUST, 1862 [6]

The night was gloomy, dark, and wet, as if we were in December. The intention of the General was to avoid every chance of a collision with the troops by marching over mountains and places inaccessible to them, and he was resolved, above all things, to decline an engagement with the Royalists under any circumstances whatever. On the 29th we knew that the troops in pursuit of us were only three miles distant. From Santa Eufemia and Palmi we received a few provisions, which were at once distributed. The General then ordered the "assembly" to be sounded, and briefly addressed us. After calling on us to support the discomforts and fatigues of long and difficult marches, he urged on all the necessity for discipline and self-denial, and then concluded with these words: "Let us trust in the justice of our cause—that which we now wish is the desire of the whole nation—it is the universal will of Italy. Let us be firm, then, and the army will be with us, and Rome will be ours." At midday, having learned that the troops were advancing against Aspromonte from Stefano, where they had passed the night, we changed our ground, and took up a position on the slope of the hill in the front of the wood of Aspromonte.

At three p.m., the troops could be seen at the extremity of the plain. We were drawn up in line, and occupied nearly the whole

[6] *The life of Garibaldi, including his career in South America, Rome, Piedmont, and Lombardy . . . interspersed with anecdotes.* Manchester, 1864, pp. 91–92.

edge of the wood looking to the east and to the south. The three battalions of *bersaglieri* formed the left and center, and the right was composed of the Corrao Brigade. General Garibaldi had selected this position, not with a view of attacking, but with the idea of avoiding any collision, believing that the orders issued against us would be more humane, and being fully persuaded that, before opening fire on us, a parley would be demanded, or that, at the least, we should be summoned to surrender. But the orders were extreme—"*to pursue us, attack us, destroy us!*" Seeing that the troops continued to advance, the "assembly" was sounded, and express orders were given to all the commanders of battalions and companies *not to fire,* and to keep their men silent and sitting on the ground. The regular troops advanced with the *bersaglieri* at their head. At three hundred paces' distance the *bersaglieri* opened out, and advanced at the double for another hundred paces. General Garibaldi and some of his staff continued to repeat the orders "*not to fire,*" as they passed in front of our line, from the center to the left. In an instant the regular troops opened fire, *directing their volleys against the General,* who, standing erect about ten paces in advance of our line, replied to the discharges of the *bersaglieri* by cries of "*Viva l'Italia!*" and by repeating the order "*not to fire*" to his own men.

At the third volley the General was wounded at the same instant in the right foot and in the left thigh. The wound in the foot was so severe as to cause him to fall, and some of his officers carried him to the rear, placing him under a tree at the edge of the wood; and there, calm and serene, he continued to cry out that the fire must not be returned, and sent officers of the staff to repeat the order, while Ripari, Basile, and myself were examining his wounds. But the Picciotti, who formed the right of the line, inflamed at the sight of their wounded companions, and weary of inaction, in direct opposition to orders, then opened fire, and replied to the fire of the troops. The moment they had fired, every bugle sounded "Cease firing," and, by a strange coincidence, as our bugles were sounding "Cease firing," those of the regular troops sounded "Advance, firing." Not a single shot was fired from our left or center, and the troops advanced without opposition, and mingled with our men. . . .

[Some of the attacking force] presented themselves with tears in their eyes to the general; many among them had served in campaigns under him, and now approached to shake hands with him in silence. One among them, a sergeant of *bersaglieri*—he was one of the "Thousand of Marsala"—knelt and begged the forgiveness of his former general. There was a circle of volunteers and regulars around the wounded man—the former bowed down with grief, as sons weeping round a father; and the second, confused and ashamed, were grieving for the crime to which they had been urged. In order to spare the blood of brothers, our staff at once treated with Colonel Pallavicini, and, without any resistance, their arms were given up by those who, on leaving home, had sworn to enter Rome or die under its walls. And those who thus calmly submitted were heroes of Rome in 1849, of '59 and of '60. We did not yield to force, but out of pity to our country; Italy will esteem this great sacrifice; and history, recording the fact, will tell how the Garibaldian volunteers of Aspromonte, rather than spill the blood of their brothers, sadly, but willingly, yielded up those arms with which they had gained so many battles.

7

Garibaldi Looks at the Outside World

Although he was a good patriot, Garibaldi had learnt from Mazzini and the Saint Simonians to feel himself also a true citizen of the world. Other oppressed nations, for instance Poland, Hungary, and Denmark, could always rely on his support. Even before Italy was recognized as a state, he was advocating the creation of a united Europe.

A FEDERATION OF EUROPE, OCTOBER, 1860 [1]

Civilization and progress are words on everyone's lips, but it seems to me that, apart from our higher standard of living, we differ little from people in those primitive times when men tore each other to pieces over their prey. We pass our time threatening each other, though most Europeans of sense and intelligence understand perfectly well that there is no need to spend our poor lives in perpetual threats and mutual hostility. There seems to exist some secret and invisible enemy which inhibits the union of peoples and forces us to kill each other with every refinement of skill.

But if only Europe formed a single state, who would there be to disturb us, and who in the outside world would threaten the peace of such a sovereign Power which would dominate the world? There would then be no more need for armies and navies, and the enormous sums now extracted from the poor in order to be spent on extermination would instead be converted to the development of industry and the advantage of everyone. . . .

The basis of such a federation would have to be France and England. If these two states could frankly and honestly agree, then Italy, Spain, Portugal, Hungary, Belgium, Switzerland, Greece and

[1] *Garibaldi, Vittorio Emanuele, Cavour, nei fasti della patria: documenti inediti,* ed. Giacomo Emilio Curàtulo, Bologna, 1911, pp. 418–19.

Macedonia would instinctively group round them. At the same time the divided and oppressed nationalities—for example the Slavs, the Celts, the Germans, Scandinavians, and that colossus Russia—none of these could afford to remain outside such a process of political regeneration. Here we have something which our present century urgently demands.

A PLEDGE, JUNE 5, 1864 [2]

When Italy has become truly independent, if ever she should then threaten the liberty of other neighboring nations, I would, albeit regretfully, without doubt be on the side of the oppressed.

SECRETARY OF STATE WILLIAM H. SEWARD TO H. S. SANFORD, U. S. MINISTER AT BRUSSELS, JULY 27, 1861

Garibaldi had a great belief in the future of the United States. As he told Karl Blind, "America should increase rather than decrease in power, so that it might act as a check and counterpoise to the aristocratic and tyrannic Powers of Europe; and that was one great reason why the leading Liberals of Europe were anxious to see the [American] Union strengthened and consolidated" (Fraser's Magazine, London, 1882, Vol. XXVI, 393). *The names of Lincoln and John Brown he took over and used in his own family. In his early days, he had applied for United States' citizenship, and, though he never completed the necessary formalities, he often claimed to be an American citizen—for example, when resisting arrest in Italy. His marriage to Anita had already shown his feelings about racial equality, and a strong conviction about slavery and emancipation was one reason for his near intervention in the American Civil War.*

I send you a copy of a correspondence which has taken place between Garibaldi and J. W. Quiggle, Esq., late consul of the United States at Antwerp.

I wish you to proceed at once and enter into communication with the distinguished Soldier of Freedom. Say to him that this government believes his services in its present contest for the unity and liberty of the American People, would be exceedingly useful, and

[2] *Edizione Nazionale degli Scritti di Giuseppe Garibaldi,* Vol. V, 237-38.

that, therefore, they are earnestly desired and invited. Tell him that this government believes he will, if possible, accept this call, because it is too certain that the fall of the American Union, if indeed it were possible, would be a disastrous blow to the cause of Human Freedom equally here, in Europe, and throughout the world.

Tell him that he will receive a Major-General's commission in the army of the United States, with its appointments, with the hearty welcome of the American People.

Tell him that we have abundant resources, and numbers unlimited at our command, and a nation resolved to remain united and free.

General Garibaldi will recognize in me, not merely an organ of the government, but an old and sincere personal friend.

SANFORD TO SEWARD, SEPTEMBER 18, 1861

I found the general still an invalid but able to leave his room, however, to which he had been confined for several months, and had on that day a long conversation with him on the subject of his going to the United States.

He said that the only way in which he could render service, as he ardently desired to do, to the cause of the United States, was as Commander-in-chief of its forces, that he would only go as such, and with the additional contingent power—to be governed by events—of declaring the abolition of slavery; that he would be of little use without the first, and without the second it would appear like a civil war in which the world at large could have little interest or sympathy. I observed to him that the President had no such powers to confer—that I was authorized to communicate with him on the subject of his letter to our consul at Antwerp confidentially, and if found acceptable to offer him a commission of Major-General, which I doubted not would carry with it the command of a large *corps d'armée* to conduct in his own way within certain limits in the prosecution of the war, and informed him of the tenor of your despatch of July 27th. As, however, I found that such position would not be acceptable it would not be in my power to make such proposition. He expressed himself flattered by your appreciation of him and grateful for the friendly sentiments manifested by the President and yourself, but said his mind was made up only to take service in the position already indicated.

GEORGE MARSH, U. S. MINISTER AT TURIN, TO SECRETARY OF STATE SEWARD, SEPTEMBER 14, 1861 [3]

Mr. Sanford arrived here from Caprera on the evening of Thursday the 12th, and left for Brussels the next morning. He will of course explain to you the causes of his failure to accomplish the object of his mission, and on that subject I need only say that his want of success is not to be ascribed to any error or indiscretion on his part. He has, in my judgment, conducted the whole affair with much prudence, tact and skill, and I am satisfied that the services of General Garibaldi cannot, under present circumstances, be secured, except by the offer of terms which Mr. Sanford was not authorized, and the American government would not be inclined, to propose.

Although, after the correspondence which had taken place between Mr. Quiggle and Garibaldi, the President could not well avoid making some advances to that distinguished soldier, I do not by any means look upon his assumption of a position which precluded all negotiation, and put it out of Mr. Sanford's power to make a proposal at all, as an evil. His constitutional independence of character and action, his long habit of exercising uncontrolled and irresponsible authority, the natural and honorable pride which he cannot but feel in reviewing his own splendid career and vast achievements, and the consciousness that though but a solitary and private individual, he is at this moment in and of himself, one of the great Powers of the world—all these combine to render it difficult if not impossible for him, consistently with due self respect, to accept such military rank and powers as the President can constitutionally and lawfully offer him. . . .

But the opinions which this remarkable man entertains with regard to the character of the contest between the federal government and the insurgent states would constitute an equally insuperable objection, in his mind, to his acceptance of a commission in the American Army, or to his usefulness in it so long as those opinions remain unchanged.

I have been for some months aware that he considers this contest a struggle in which no important political or philanthropic principle is involved, thinks the parties are contending about purely ma-

[3] This and the two preceding letters from *The Century Magazine*, New York, November, 1907, Vol. LXXV, 67–70, letters edited by Nelson Gay.

terial interests, and holds that neither of them has superior claims upon the sympathies of the European friends of liberty and of progress. Garibaldi has never been ambitious of wielding power or winning laurels in a cause which did not commend itself to him as something more than a question of legal right and governmental interests, and this the cause of the American government and union, as regarded from his point of view, has thus far failed to do. He, as his friends represent, does not think that the perpetuity and extension of domestic slavery constitute one of the issues of the war, and though I should not be surprised if, in spite of what has passed between him and Mr. Sanford, he should visit America of his own motion, with a view of examining the position of affairs on the spot, yet I do not believe he will take any part in the struggle, unless he is convinced that the government and the people of the North are united in the determination to pursue a policy which shall necessarily result in the abolition of slavery.

LETTER TO ABRAHAM LINCOLN, AUGUST 6, 1863 [4]

In the midst of your titanic struggle, permit me, as another among the free children of Columbus, to send you a word of greeting and admiration for the great work you have begun. Posterity will call you the great emancipator, a more enviable title than any crown could be, and greater than any merely mundane treasure. You are a true heir of the teaching given us by Christ and by [John] Brown. If an entire race of human beings, subjugated into slavery by human egoism, has been restored to human dignity, to civilization and human love, this is by your doing and at the price of the most noble lives in America.

It is America, the same country which taught liberty to our forefathers, which now opens another solemn epoch of human progress. And while your tremendous courage astonishes the world, we are sadly reminded how this old Europe, which also can boast a great cause of liberty to fight for, has not found the mind or heart to equal you.

A BANQUET GIVEN FOR GARIBALDI IN LONDON, 1864 [5]

The English had a very special regard for Garibaldi. In 1854, the working men of Newcastle had subscribed to give

[4] *Giuseppe Garibaldi, Scritti politici e militari,* ed. Domenico Ciàmpoli, Rome, 1907, Vol. I, 330.
[5] *The Times,* London, April 14, 1864, p. 14.

*him a present; in 1861, 17,000 inhabitants of Brighton con-
tributed a penny each to make him another; and these were
typical of many such instances. Very large sums were forthcoming to assist his Sicilian expedition, and it was a source of
dismay to the organizers of his campaign that more financial
support seemed to be forthcoming from England than Italy.
Queen Victoria strongly disapproved when her eldest son
secretly went to visit Garibaldi; but she herself, though out-
wardly censorious, privately sent to beg him for the gift of a
signed photograph.*

*Garibaldi's visit to England, in 1864, marked the highest
point in his popularity, and his uprorious reception there was
strongly resented in official Italian circles. At Portsmouth, he
inspected the British fleet. In the Isle of Wight, he was welcomed by Tennyson. Crowds waited to greet him at each railway station, and, when he reached London, he received what
the* Daily Telegraph *called "the most memorable ovation that
has ever been given at any period of the world's history."
Garibaldi never courted popular ovations, but took this very
much in his stride; he would hardly have been human not to
welcome it as an approval of what he stood for. It was a spon-
taneous demonstration by an estimated 600,000 people in the
streets of the largest city in the world. No King, no Emperor,
had ever been accorded such a triumph, anywhere.*

*Apart from this popular acclaim, the London aristocracy
took enthusiasm to extravagant lengths. They were not to
know that Garibaldi had already broken off one engagement
to an English lady because of her liking for the boring ban-
quets and receptions to which he was now once again sub-
jected* ad nauseam. *He himself behaved almost impeccably
in what must have been trying and difficult circumstances.
Forced to make many speeches, he bravely used to speak in
English, and his pronouncements on politics were judicious
and moderate. Yet he did not let political considerations deter
him from a generous greeting to his old mentor and adver-
sary, Mazzini. He also called personally on Alexander Herzen,
Louis Blanc, Ledru-Rollin and Karl Blind, the revolutionary
leaders who were exiled in London.*

In the evening [of April 13] the Duke and Duchess of Sutherland gave a magnificent banquet at Stafford House. Covers were

laid for 40 persons, among whom were the Duchess Dowager of Sutherland, the Duke and Duchess of Argyll [he was a cabinet minister], the Marchioness of Ely, Earl and Countess Russell [he was the Foreign Minister], the Earl and Countess of Clarendon [he was a cabinet minister], the Earl and Countess of Derby [he was a former Prime Minister], the Earl and Lady Constance Grosvenor, the Earl and Countess of Malmesbury [he was a former Foreign Minister], the Earl and Countess of Shaftesbury, Viscount and Viscountess Palmerston [he was now Prime Minister], Lord and Lady Taunton, Lord and Lady Dufferin, Lord and Lady Blantyre, the Right Hon. W. E. and Mrs. Gladstone [he was Chancellor of the Exchequer]. Baron Marochetti, General Eber, Mr. Panizzi, Mr. Menotti and Mr. Ricciotti Garibaldi, Lord Albert Leveson Gower, Lord Ronald Levenson Gower, Dr. Quin, Dr. Guerzoni, and the Doctor [Bertani] and Private Secretary of General Garibaldi.

During dinner the full band of the Grenadier Guards, stationed in the grand staircase, performed a varied selection of music.

Later in the evening the Duchess gave an assembly, when the picture gallery, the great drawing-room, and the whole of the magnificent saloons which are without an equal in England, were thrown open for the reception of company. The assembly on this occasion was a truly representative one, the foremost in each grade of society being invited. Among the guests were: the Turkish Ambassador and Mme. Musurus, the American Minister [the other foreign ambassadors, including the Italian ambassador, boycotted Garibaldi's visit], Prince Edmund de Polignac, the Duke of Devonshire and Lady Louisa Cavendish, the Duke of Leinster, the Duke of St. Albans, the Duchess of St. Albans and Lady Diana Beauclerk, Viscount Falkland, the Duke of Wellington, the Duchess Dowager of Norfolk, the Duke and Duchess of Somerset and Lady Gwendolin St. Maur, the Marquis and Marchioness of Lansdowne, the Marquis and Marchioness of Salisbury, the Marquis and Marchioness of Carmarthen, the Marquis of Hartington, the Marquis and Marchioness of Clanricarde, the Marquis Balbe, Maria Marchioness of Ailesbury, the Marquis and Marchioness of Ailesbury, the Marquis Caracciolo, the Marquis and Marchioness of Westminster and Lady Theodora Grosvenor, the Countess of Westmoreland and Lady Rose Fane [and 164 more titled names, with hundreds of lesser gentry down to Sir Edwin Landseer, and mere commoners such as Mr. Cobden and Mr. Bright. All of them had come to meet and honor Garibaldi.].

GARIBALDI DINES WITH HERZEN, THE RUSSIAN
REVOLUTIONARY, NEAR LONDON, APRIL 17, 1864 [6]

Then Garibaldi rose, and with a glass of Marsala in his hand said:

> I want today to do a duty which I ought to have done long ago. Among us here is a man who has performed the greatest services both to my native land and to freedom in general. When I was a lad and was full of vague longings I sought a man to be my guide, the counsellor of my youth, I sought him as a thirsty man seeks water. I found him. He alone kept watch when all around were sleeping; he became my friend and has remained my friend for ever; in him the holy fire of love for fatherland and freedom has never dimmed; that man is Giuseppe Mazzini—I drink to him, to my friend, to my teacher!

In the voice, in the expression of face with which these words were uttered, there was so much that gripped and thrilled the heart that they were received not with applause but with tears.

After a momentary silence Garibaldi continued with the words:

> Mazzini has said a few words of unhappy Poland with which I am in complete sympathy.
>
> To Poland the land of martyrs, to Poland facing death for independence and setting a grand example to the peoples!
>
> Now let us drink to young Russia, which is suffering and struggling as we are, and like us will be victorious; to the new people which, vanquishing tsarist Russia and winning its freedom, is evidently summoned to play a great part in the destinies of Europe.
>
> And finally to England, the land of freedom and independence, the land which for its hospitality and sympathy with the persecuted deserves our fullest gratitude; to England, which gives us the possibility of a friendly gathering like this.

[6] Alexander Herzen, *My Past and Thoughts,* trans. Constance Garnett, revised by Humphrey Higgens (London: Chatto & Windus Ltd.; New York: Alfred A. Knopf, 1968), Vol. III, 1276–77. (Herzen is quoting passages which appeared in *The Bell,* No. 184, May 1, 1864.) Reprinted with the permission of Chatto & Windus Ltd. and Alfred A. Knopf Inc.

VIEWS ON GERMANY: LETTER TO KARL BLIND,
APRIL 10, 1865 [7]

The progress of humanity seems to have come to a halt, and you with your superior intelligence will know why. The reason is that the world lacks a nation which possesses true leadership. Such leadership, of course, is required not to dominate other peoples, but to lead them along the path of duty, to lead them toward the brotherhood of nations where all the barriers erected by egoism will be destroyed. We need the kind of leadership which, in the true tradition of medieval chivalry, would devote itself to redressing wrongs, supporting the weak, sacrificing momentary gains and material advantage for the much finer and more satisfying achievement of relieving the suffering of our fellow men. We need a nation courageous enough to give us a lead in this direction. It would rally to its cause all those who are suffering wrong or who aspire to a better life, and all those who are now enduring foreign oppression.

This role of world leadership, left vacant as things are today, might well be occupied by the German nation. You Germans, with your grave and philosophic character, might well be the ones who could win the confidence of others and guarantee the future stability of the international community. Let us hope, then, that you can use your energy to overcome the moth-eaten thirty tyrants of the various German states. Let us hope that in the center of Europe you can then make a unified nation out of your fifty millions. All the rest of us would eagerly and joyfully follow you.

[7] *British Museum, MSS.,* 40124 f. 323.

8
Last Thoughts on Politics and War

All was forgiven Garibaldi when another war of liberation against Austria broke out in 1866. Once again he had a chance to test his precepts about guerrilla fighting. Once again he emerged with more credit from this war than the generals and admirals of the regular forces. The latter only lost battles; he and his irregulars won them. Yet the government again gave him only inferior equipment, and refused to let him carry out the fast-moving war that he wanted.

The German General Staff, it is interesting to note, had a far higher appreciation of his military worth. The Italian Generals, on the other hand, were still deeply jealous of his successes in 1860; they also feared that the volunteer principle, like the Landwehr or militia system that Garibaldi so admired in Germany, would be a dangerous threat to themselves and the professional soldiers in the army; and, in any case, they lacked the imagination or skill to rise above the laborious, text-book tactics that they had learned at school.

Garibaldi advanced up the Alpine valleys until almost within sight of Trent, but several defeats on other more important fronts compelled the government to make peace. When ordered to withdraw he obeyed, but he fiercely blamed the politicians for signing a dishonorable armistice. He also blamed the "Italian" inhabitants of the Trentino when they showed little enthusiasm for being delivered from the hated foreigner.

INSTRUCTIONS FOR THE VOLUNTEERS IN THE TRENTINO, JULY, 1866 [1]

1) Every regiment should include a company of commandos.

[1] *Edizione Nazionale degli Scritti di Giuseppe Garibaldi*, Vol. V, 286–88, 294–96, 313–14.

2) These should be chosen from the bravest and most agile among officers and men.

3) Each regiment should have a reserve company, made up of those who are least apt for quick marches. . . .

5) The leaders of these commando groups should carry enough money to pay for food and other necessaries, and must do everything possible to see that their men behave well toward the local inhabitants.

6) They should employ two good guides chosen from among these inhabitants.

7) The main job of each commando will be to molest the enemy in whatever way possible, cutting railways and electric cables, and destroying whatever they find that belongs to the enemy. . . .

10) Marching by night and resting by day is the best way of concealing your position, and each dawn should find you somewhere unexpected. . . .

12) You should never engage superior forces if you can help it, but always do your utmost to remain masters of the battlefield, as it is a terrible thing to abandon one's wounded to the enemy.

13) If nothing else is possible, you must keep the enemy awake by continuous shooting at night. . . .

17) Volunteers must be careful not to fall into the error of fearing cavalry, especially in broken country. Operating in tree-covered territory you are more than a match for mounted enemy patrols. Be also on guard against those shameful moments of panic which are so frequent with young soldiers. If panic starts, the braver men should kick some sense into those overcome with fear. Officers and experienced soldiers should have explained to recruits about former encounters so as to put them on their guard against these two dangers. . . .

22) In mountain territory, commandos should be careful not to attack enemy strongpoints without first establishing control over the surrounding heights. . . .

23) It is always better to attack in open order rather than in solid groups, except in very special cases. . . .

29) Commanders must understand that we shall never be able to serve the holy cause of our country if provisions are not assured ahead of time. The Intendant General therefore has orders that every column should have cattle allocated to it for the provision of meat rations. . . .

31) Where the roads are poor and means of transport lacking,

one must march more lightly than usual and not exceed the two baggage wagons per battalion as laid down by regulations. . . .

42) Officers should be assiduous in the moral instruction of their men, personally taking over the discussions in camp and explaining the reasons for each victory or defeat. They must explain that brave people are always victorious and suffer few casualties, whereas those who flee from the enemy are much more easily picked off.

PROPOSALS PUT TO AN INTERNATIONAL CONGRESS FOR PEACE AT GENEVA, 1867 [2]

It was to all appearances more than a little incongruous that, between his military campaigns of 1866 and 1867, Garibaldi should have been the main guest at a Congress of Peace at Geneva; nevertheless, he was quite genuinely beginning to turn against war as a means of solving the world's problems. He reminded his hearers at Geneva that the Crimean War had sacrificed a quarter of a million men over what was basically a squabble between different Christian faiths that could not agree about the Holy Places at Jerusalem. He apologized to the Congress that the proposals he submitted to them had been hurriedly written and might not all seem relevant to the occasion, but they must bear with him because of the strength of his feelings.

Rome and the Papacy were now his main target, for, without Rome, Italy was still incomplete. He wanted the religion of Torquemada and the Holy Inquisition to yield place to a more tolerant and less totalitarian "religion of Christ." There should be a "priesthood of the Leibnitzes, the Galileos, the Keplers, the Aragos, the Newtons, the Quinets, the Rousseaus, etc. And we shall thus have cleared the path which will conduct us to the fraternity of nations, and cement in a durable manner the pact of universal peace" (The Times, *London, September 14, 1867, p. 12*).

1. All nations should be regarded as sisters.
2. War between them should be thought of as impossible.
3. All international quarrels ought to be decided by a Congress.

[2] Giuseppe Guerzoni, *Garibaldi: con documenti editi e inediti,* Florence, 1882, Vol. II, 485.

4. The members of this Congress should be democratically elected.

5. All peoples, however small, should have the right to representation in this Congress.

6. The papacy, being the most harmful of all secret societies, ought to be abolished.

7. I propose that this present Congress should formally adhere to the religion of God, by which I mean those elements of religion that are demonstrably true and reasonable, and we should pledge ourselves to propagate it.

8. The priesthood of revelation and of ignorance should be replaced by one of wisdom and intelligence.

9. Democracy alone can put an end to wars.

10. The only legitimate wars are those where a tyrant is opposed by those he has enslaved.

THE PREFACE TO GARIBALDI'S FIRST NOVEL, 1869 [3]

In retirement, Garibaldi turned his attention to writing three novels, as well as further instalments of autobiography. He also spoke out from time to time on politics. For awhile, he tried to weld together the many small groups on the political Left, but their fissiparous tendencies proved too much for him. Always honest, his own political views were simple, sometimes muddled, sometimes potentially dangerous, and sometimes both advanced and sensible. He campaigned for universal suffrage, for female emancipation, for reduced taxes on the poor, and for reduced expenditure on the army. His concern for public health made him interested in land reclamation; hence, he busied himself with the question of planting eucalyptus trees and reviving cotton cultivation. With the support of English engineers, he put forward to parliament a scheme for draining the Pontine marshes by diverting the River Tiber and creating an artificial port at Fiumicino. He also developed an interest in socialism, and hundreds of the first working men's unions made him their honorary president.

My first reason for writing a novel is to remind Italy of those brave men who fell on the field of battle for her sake. Some of their

[3] Giuseppe Garibaldi, *Clelia, ovvero il governo del monaco, romanzo storico-politico*, Milan, 1870, pp. i–ii.

names are well known, but many are not, and their remembrance is a sacred duty for me.

Secondly I want to appeal directly to the youth of Italy. I want to put before them the deeds which other young Italians have done, and remind them of their duty to finish the task. In particular I want to point out the base and deceitful conduct of governments and priests.

In the third place I need to earn some money. Better do something than nothing, and the idleness which circumstances have forced on me I find oppressive.

Most of my writing will be about people who are dead, for I agree with the old saying that it is hard to judge men when they are alive. Tired of the realities of this life, I turn with the greater pleasure to historical novels. The historical part I think I can vouch for, though no historical events are ever completely known, and to narrate military events with real precision is notoriously hard.

As to the non-historical part—well, if my aim were not to embellish real events, and if I were not moved by the desire to expose the vices and wickedness of the priests, I would not have bored the public when there are writers alive such as Manzoni, Guerrazzi and Victor Hugo.

AN APPEAL FOR ITALY, IN AN ENGLISH NEWSPAPER, 1870 [4]

Unhappy people! who might so easily have been regenerated, and who could have taken so honorable a place at the great banquet of nations!—for, let me assure you, Englishmen, the Italian people are good people, easily led right, and capable of high enthusiasm in the cause of progress. But what can you expect? Who troubles his head about them? Those spoliators of the public money who call themselves the government have other things to think about. Their minds are intent upon amassing sufficient money to pay a whole host of parasites who sap the life of the nation, and the wretched masses of the people are left to groan on in their ignorance and misery. . . .

The States (past and present) of the Pope, and also those of Sardinia, are, like the Two Sicilies, in a truly pitiable plight. The Northern States are not quite so badly off; but as far as the country people are concerned, I may say that everywhere, without exception —and you may believe it on my authority—we are still in the Mid-

⁴ *Cassell's Magazine,* London, 1870, pp. 504, 543.

dle Ages; and that any fanatic with a crucifix in his hand might preach with success a general crusade against the Liberals, and sanctify in Italy the most holy and blessed cause of the Inquisition. . . .

The crime committed by the brigands has suggested, or rather recalled, to me my views on the general bearing of those governments which are called civilized, and which, rightly considered, are quite otherwise. They themselves are doubtless the cause of that Babylonian anarchy which makes Europe the battle-field for a perpetual strife between misery and luxury, between the oppressed and the oppressors. Who will deny that the prime cause of brigandage in Italy is Bonaparte [Louis Napoleon], with the priests for his myrmidons and the Italian Government for his accomplices? Does not this son of Hortense, with his crocodile's devotion, bring about the misery of my country by maintaining in the heart of Italy that den of assassins [i.e. the Papal States], which not only serves as a refuge for the brigands, but is, as it were, the hive whence issues that swarm of false teachers who infest Central and Southern Italy? . . . .

What shall we say of those millions of men snatched away in the midst of their youth and vigor from the workshop and the plough, to guard a few families in luxury and tranquillity—families, the origin of whose power and immense riches is such, that if there were justice on the earth they could not be named in the same breath with those brigands of Greece and Italy? Why do not those European governments who arm themselves to the teeth that they may bring misery on the nations, unite to disarm these useless and harmful masses which ruin and oppress the world—to employ the millions necessary for their maintenance in improving and educating the poor? Misery and ignorance, these are the origin of brigandage—in other words, despotism and a bigoted priesthood. Those noble victims to Greek brigandage, and those who fall a prey every day to Italian brigandage, must be added to the huge column of debts which European despotism for ever contracts with humanity.

Let England appeal to those nations who can act for themselves, such as the United States, Switzerland, Belgium (perhaps) , etc., to join in laying the foundations of one universal union. All the lesser Powers will certainly find it their interest to join the union, and sooner or later the greater ones, impelled by subjects weary of aristocratic brigandage, will come to take their places in it.

1. War an impossibility. 2. All differences between the nations to

be judged by the congress. As the result of these wise and happy deliberations, we shall then have an international army and fleet sufficient to free the world from brigands and pirates, without being obliged to make war on the suffering classes for the mere pleasure of their masters, as it unhappily occurs every day.

THOUGHTS ON SOCIALISM, NOVEMBER, 1871 [5]

If you ask me whether I understand the socialist International, I answer you frankly that I have belonged to my idea of an International ever since I served the republics of the Rio Grande and Montevideo, in other words long before it ever became a formally established society in Europe. In France, during the war of 1870–1871, I publicly subscribed to the International. Furthermore in February 1871, when I left the Bordeaux Assembly, if I had known then what was about to happen, I would have gone to fight in Paris for the commune, in other words for the cause of justice against the injustice of the doctrinaires. The poor people of Paris were then being crushed by that odd amalgam of monarchists, priests and unworthy generals.

What I oppose in the International, just as I oppose the same thing in monarchism, is where it becomes cruel and inhumane. Anyone who spends his life starving the poor so that rich prelates could live well ought to be imprisoned, and yet I am equally against those archimandrites of international socialism who talk about property being theft, or about inheritance and capitalism being inherently wicked.

I hold no position in the International, and the fact that I am known not to approve all their program might be a reason for them excluding me. My idea of it is of a force making for the moral and material improvement of the honest working classes. . . . A fourth estate is emerging today which, if well organized, may be able to bring together workers from both town and countryside. Difficult though this be, if it succeeded it would carry all before it. No doubt it could be delayed by imprisoning some of its leaders and exiling others, but I think it should and will succeed. And is it not better in that case to help such a strong association toward a good end rather than a bad? Is it not better to do what one can to help other wise and honest men keep it on the right lines?

[5] Letter of November 14, 1871, to Giorgio Pallavicino: *Giuseppe Garibaldi, Scritti politici e militari*, ed. Domenico Ciàmpoli, Rome, 1907, Vol. II, 599–600.

POLITICAL PROGRAM, JUNE, 1873 [6]

Our policy should be the abolition of every law which hinders the progress and welfare of ordinary citizens, and hence the common people should have some say in law-making.

The Church should be disestablished and not joined to the State. The educational system should, in matters of religion, be neutral.

Permanent armies should be abolished, and instead there should be a period of military service for everyone.

Titles and privileges should be abolished, both those of birth and those acquired by property ownership.

The organization of labor should be entrusted to the State, to be used for the material and intellectual advancement of the workers.

Elementary education should be obligatory and free, and so should technical schools. We ought to have universal suffrage.

We also need to have just a single tax, and it ought to be proportional to the wealth of each citizen.

THOUGHTS ON DICTATORSHIP AND DEMOCRACY, APRIL, 1871 [7]

Garibaldi was an unabashed advocate of what he called "temporary, benevolent dictatorship" during emergency conditions such as those of the risorgimento; and, when the fighting was over, he still looked upon a government with emergency powers as about the only hope for abating privilege and introducing genuine social reforms. This was an ingenuous belief and a perilous one. It should, however, be remembered that his first request for the appointment of a temporary dictator was in June, 1849, when supreme powers were needed for the defence of Rome; that the second was in anticipation of the war against Austria, in 1859; the third was in May, 1860, when he had to create a war-time government in Sicily; and the fourth was in April, 1871, when he advised the Paris Commune that their revolution would need emergency powers if it were to survive.

In the context of these occasions, there was something to be said for his views. Garibaldi was correct in believing that the

[6] Enrico Emilio Ximenes, *Epistolario di Giuseppe Garibaldi*, Milan, 1885, Vol. II, 46–47.
[7] *The Echo*, London, April 20, 1871.

Italian parliamentary system had little to do with democracy. His own experience in the House of Deputies in April 1861, and in the French assembly at Bordeaux in March 1871, convinced him that these parliaments were a good deal less liberal than many liberals liked to think.

Dictatorship, like Machiavellianism, has been wrongly understood. Machiavelli, one of our greatest Italians, did but exhibit vice; he never counselled it. The fact that Sulla and Caesar were dictators, should but teach us to seek the more diligently for a Cincinnatus and a Washington. If a Bonaparte can corrupt, so much the worse for those who are corrupted. Ancient Rome, when republican and virtuous (which are but synonyms), finding herself in distress, sought out a man, and that man saved the republic.

Is it not easier to find one honest man than to find five hundred? [i.e., in a parliament] And honesty, I fear, is not too abundant in these present times.

What France wants is a chief; she has those equal to the task among her citizens, but she does not seek them. Why? Because she prefers assemblies, committees—in one word, Byzantinism. You may answer me by saying that the government of France is even now in the hands of one, namely, Thiers. But Thiers! What is he but the head of French chauvinism? The man who would establish the greatness of France upon the abasement and misfortune of her neighbors is but a wretch.

Democracy is always weak in the face of despotism, from want of concentrated power.

POLITICAL TESTAMENT [8]

To my children and friends, and to whoever may share my views, I bequeath my love for Liberty and the Truth, and my hatred for all lies and tyranny. . . .

To my fellow citizens I recommend that they should consider the purist and exclusive republicans of Mazzini's school as harmful to Italy, as little better than the moderates, or indeed than the priests.

However bad the present government of Italy may be, it will not be easy to overthrow it, and I therefore advocate the view of Dante

---

[8] *Edizione Nazionale degli Scritti di Giuseppe Garibaldi,* Bologna, 1937, Vol. VI, 316–18.

that if necessary we must work with the devil himself if that is best for the national interest.

Whatever happens we must accept things as they are. For instance we must not overspend our income, or else ruin is sure. . . .

Once Italy is master of herself, she should if possible proclaim herself a republic, but not entrust her fate to five hundred lawyers [i.e., parliament] who will first deafen her with talk and then lead her to destruction. Instead, the most honest man among Italians should be selected as a temporary dictator with the same powers as once were wielded by a Fabius or a Cincinnatus. This dictatorial system would have to last until Italians were more educated to liberty than at present and until her existence was no longer threatened by powerful neighbors.

PART TWO

GARIBALDI THROUGH THE EYES
OF HIS CONTEMPORARIES

9
In South America, 1836-48

Garibaldi's first serious military campaigns were on behalf of the Rio Grande, against the "Portuguese imperialism" of Brazil. He then fought for the colorados *of the Banda Oriental (Uruguay), against the* blancos *of the Argentine. Rosas, dictator of the Argentine, was jealous of the commercial prosperity of Uruguay, and in an attempt to dominate the whole estuary of the River Plate spent ten years blockading Montevideo by sea and land. Many foreigners lived in the besieged town, and a French Legion was recruited for its defense; there was also an Italian Legion under Garibaldi, and here the famous red shirt first made its appearance on the* colorado *side.*

Some of the Uruguayans were jealous of this guerrilla leader from overseas. The Irish commander of the Argentinian navy also made unconfirmed but not implausible complaints against the Italian Legion for their cruelty and for sacking harmless villages (Enrique Arana, *Rosas en la Evolución Política Argentina, Buenos Aires, 1954, Vol. II, 87*). But such criticisms were the exception. For the space of two years, Garibaldi was under the orders of senior French and British officers, and their testimony agreed that even at this early period he was a truly remarkable man. Lord Howden in the British House of Lords remembered him as "a disinterested individual among those who only sought their own personal advantage . . . a person of great courage and military skill" (Hansard's Parliamentary Debates, *July 10, 1849, Vol. CVII,*

94). *Admiral Lainé, Sir William Gore Ouseley, and the future Admiral Winnington-Ingram confirmed this opinion. "Our Garibaldi," wrote Mazzini with pride, in 1846, "now possesses a name whose glory we must spread among the youth of Italy"* (Scritti editi ed inediti di Giuseppe Mazzini, Imola, 1943, appendice, Vol. VI, 505).

ALEXANDRE DUMAS ON GARIBALDI IN SOUTH AMERICA [1]

Among those who led the defense of Montevideo, and who earned the gratitude not only of this one town but of the whole Uruguayan nation, there is above all others the name of José Garibaldi. An exile from Italy where he had fought for liberty; exiled from France for the same reason; exiled again from Brazil after he had lent his help in the foundation of the Rio Grande Republic, he then volunteered for the service of Montevideo. I should like to tell people about this valorous man, whose conduct no critics have been able to impugn without damaging their own reputations.

Garibaldi was then a man of 38, of medium height, well-proportioned, with fair hair, blue eyes, a Greek nose and a Greek chin and forehead—features which in general are classical in their beauty. His beard is long. Normally he wears a close-fitting coat which has nothing of a military uniform about it. His movements are graceful. His voice has a splendid and melodious softness. For the most part he seems absent-minded and a person of more imagination than calculation; but, once mention the word independence, or that of Italy, and he becomes a volcano in eruption. He never carries arms except in battle; but when the moment arrives he takes up the first sword which comes to hand, throwing away the scabbard and proceeding at once to attack.

In 1842, put in charge of the small Montevidean navy, he led an expedition up the river Paranà to fight a bitter campaign against three times as many men. When resistance was no longer possible, he ran his tiny ships aground and burnt them. Then he led their crews back to help in the defense of Montevideo. He and the war minister, Pacheco y Obes, at once understood each other and formed a quite unusually true and close friendship. Not only besieged, but blockaded by the navy of Rosas, the defense had to be carried on at sea as well as on land, and the minister, with Garibaldi's help,

[1] Alexandre Dumas (*père*), *Montevideo ou une nouvelle Troie*, Paris, 1850, pp. 84–91.

was able after two months to put four small ships into action carrying the Uruguayan flag against the navy of Rosas under Admiral Brown. . . .

On February 8, 1846 [after also forming the Italian Legion to help with the land defenses], Garibaldi led two hundred of these Italians to engage an Argentinian force of 1,200 under General Servando Gomez. How did he meet this situation? The bravest people could hardly have been expected to do more here than to make the best of any defensive position, but in fact he attacked with his 200 against 1,200, and after five bitter hours of fighting he had destroyed the enemy infantry and even forced their demoralized cavalry to retreat, leaving himself in charge of the battlefield.

Always in the thick of any battle, once the fighting was over he did his best to mitigate the harsh consequences of war. If he was ever seen in the government offices, it was just to ask for pardon on behalf of a condemned man or a favor for someone who had suffered misfortune. Because of his intervention, Don Miguel Molina y Haedo had his life spared in 1844 after being tried and condemned. At Gualeguaychu he captured Colonel Villagra, one of the most ferocious of Rosas' officers, but at once set him and his companions free. At Ytapevy he captured Colonel Lavalleja's family after a successful fight, but then sent these prisoners back to the Colonel with a courteous and generous letter.

It should be repeated that Garibaldi lived at Montevideo with his family in the most extreme poverty. He had no other footwear than his military boots, and often his friends had to use subterfuge to replace his old torn clothes with new ones.

If only those newspaper correspondents who have called Garibaldi a military adventurer or *condottiere* would write to Montevideo and ask politicians and merchants about him, or would enquire of ordinary citizens, they would discover that no one in this republic has enjoyed more universal honor and esteem than he.

RECOLLECTIONS OF THE RIVER PLATE BY A BRITISH NAVAL OFFICER [2]

Garibaldi had gained the sobriquet of "El diavolo" from the Blancos [of Argentina], as they believed him to be ubiquitous, and for this reason: often, after one of these dashing attacks before Mon-

---

[2] Rear-Admiral H. F. Winnington-Ingram, *Hearts of Oak*, London, 1889, pp. 92–93.

tevideo, he would, in the evening, when his movements were screened by the shadows of night, embark with some hundred of his followers on board a fast-sailing schooner, and, landing either at St. Lucia or Colonia—places higher up the river in Orientali [Uruguayan] territory, and also besieged by the armies of Rosas—perform the same kind of feat at the outposts of these towns as we have just described him doing at the capital.

Garibaldi's name had become a tower of strength to the Colorado cause, for it had already carried terror to the ears of the Imperial Brazilian forces in the Rio Grande do Sul, a neighbouring province to the Banda Oriental that had risen in insurrection a few years previously. Garibaldi, as an exile from his native Genoa, had, up to that period, led the peaceful life of the master of a trading coaster in these regions; but the generous spirit which urged him in after days to the relief of oppressed nationalities was only dormant within him, and waiting a fitting opportunity. It came at Porto Alegre, in the Rio Grande.

A strong Spanish element existed in that province, and it was not disposed to settle down quietly under Portuguese Imperialism when their co-patriots a few miles farther south were enjoying republican institutions. They, therefore, rose to arms to free themselves from Brazilian rule. Trade was paralyzed from this cause, and the future hero of Rome and Marsala must have found it difficult to dispose of his cargo, and thus he was placed in enforced idleness, which is said to be the parent of mischief; be this so or not, it was evident that Garibaldi's warrior instincts could no longer be restrained, and he entered boldly into the conflict, which eventually drained the resources of the Empire before it could become the victor.

Whilst engaged in this strife Garibaldi wooed and won the beautiful Anita, a creole born, but with all the engaging manners of the señoritas of old Spain. She had become, from the habits of her country, a splendid horsewoman, and it was a sight to be remembered as she rode a curveting animal by the side of her husband, when the Italian band played his legion home from their day's duty at the outer lines of Montevideo to the plaza in the city, where they were dismissed to their respective billets. Garibaldi was at this time in the full vigor of manhood, with a firm well-knit frame which sat his horse like a centaur. He wore his hair and beard long; they were then of a dark brown color, with a reddish tint in the latter. His countenance was remarkable for its serenity, and the lips pressed close together denoted a strong will, whilst his eyes were steadfast and piercing in their gaze. In stature he was of medium height, and was altogether the *beau ideal* of a chief of irregular troops. His scarlet tunic fitted loosely to the body, and round its collar was tied the two ends of a gaudy handkerchief, which lay unfolded on the back of the uniform. His cavalry sword-belt confined the dress to the waist, and in his saddle-holsters were a pair of pistols. On his head was the same description of black felt hat and feather as worn by all his corps.

In regard to the origin of the Garibaldian red shirt, its adoption was caused by the necessity of clothing as economically as possible the newly-raised legion, and a liberal offer having been made by a mercantile house in Montevideo to sell to the Government, at reduced prices, a stock of red woollen shirts that had been intended for the Buenos Ayres market, which was now closed by the blockade established there, it was thought too good a chance to be neglected, and the purchase was, therefore, effected. These goods were intended to be worn by those employed in the "Saladéros," or great slaughtering and salting establishments for cattle at Enseñada and other places in the Argentine provinces, as they made good winter clothing, and by their color disguised in a measure the bloody work the men had in hand.

WILLIAM GORE OUSELEY, BRITISH MINISTER IN URUGUAY, 1845–47 [3]

While employed as special Minister at Montevideo, I was for about two years in constant communication with this remarkable man. He was, as Commander in Chief of the Montevidean naval force, placed by that government under the orders of the English and French Admirals. The vessels of the combined English and French squadrons were for the most part of too great a draft of water to serve in some of the tributaries of the River Plate, and the Montevidean flotilla was found of the greatest use on many occasions in defending the Banda Oriental from repeated invasions by Rosas' forces. In order to render the flotilla efficient it was necessary to supply Garibaldi with arms, munitions of war, naval stores, or the means of procuring them. . . .

[3] "Garibaldi in South America: A New Document," ed. G. M. Trevelyan, *The Cornhill Magazine*, March, 1911, London, XXX, 392–94.

Encouraged by the reputation that even at that time Garibaldi had acquired, not merely for gallantry in arms but for honor and integrity, I resolved on making all arrangements with himself personally. Of course at first, and while I had little knowledge or experience of this deserving man, a certain degree of distrust induced me to take various methods of checking his accounts, and indirectly ascertaining that the supplies were duly administered. Nothing could be more satisfactory than the results of my examination, and even of investigations hostile in their character, and called for by persons anxious to be themselves employed in these matters and extremely jealous of Garibaldi as a foreigner, and both nationally and personally interested in opposing him. Every test redounded to his honor, and further experience showed the excellence of his judgment, and the prudence of his advice. Indeed the French and English Admirals had more than once to regret having at first distrusted and rejected his counsels.

Garibaldi used to come to me generally in the evening, and always enveloped in a poncho or cloak, which garment he never quitted while the interview lasted. This appeared singular. I subsequently ascertained that his reason for coming after dark was that he had not means to purchase lights for his own use, and therefore he wrote and prepared his orders, maps, etc., as long as daylight lasted, and then came to me. He wore his poncho to conceal the dilapidated state of his clothes, for he literally had not wherewithal to procure a decent suit. The pay and rations that he ought to have received from the government of Montevideo never reached him, or only a trifling part of them. The necessities of the government often left all payments unavoidably much in arrear, for the interior of the Banda Oriental was occupied almost entirely by the besieging troops of Rosas. . . .

At this very time, and while Garibaldi was almost in a state of destitution, Rosas made the most pressing overtures to him—offering him not only the command of the Buenos Ayrean flotilla, with considerable appointments, but a present of 30,000 hard dollars, to be paid immediately. But the proffered temptation had not the slightest effect on Garibaldi, who retained his command during my stay in the River Plata, and after I had been superseded by Lord Howden, who subsequently expressed in the House of Lords a very favorable opinion of Garibaldi.

An exceptional and most useful qualification possessed by Garibaldi is that he is able to command and act, afloat as well as on shore, being an excellent practical seaman, with much nautical knowledge. The Genoese and Sardinians, then under his command, partook of this quality, although they were by habit more sailors than soldiers. I could relate many traits of the daring of this gallant leader, as well as of his prudence and skill.

The extreme modesty of his quiet and rather reserved manners strikes those who see him for the first time, and who in most instances have previously formed a totally erroneous opinion of him. Kind, humane and gentle as he is disposed to be, he knows how to keep his followers in order, and to exact obedience. He not only never was known to avail himself of his many opportunities of even allowable personal profit, and has always strictly prevented his men from pillaging or otherwise misconducting themselves.

AN ITALIAN FRIEND COMMENTS ON GARIBALDI'S EARLY EDUCATION [4]

I once heard one of Garibaldi's friends and fellow-soldiers recall the fact that, as a young man, he knew by heart all the basic theorems of geometry. No doubt we should not attribute too much importance to such a feat of memory, yet it should remind us that he was a sea captain, and the acquisition of his captain's certificate proves that he knew a good bit about mathematics, astronomy, physical geography, commercial law and so forth. His long, difficult, and successful voyages are further proof that he did possess such knowledge. . . .

Not only this, but no one can deny that he had some awareness of literature, even if it was perhaps a bit muddled, even odd, and in general undigested and disorganized. On the deck of his ship at the age of twenty-seven he used to write poems, which, even though they would not promote him to the heights of the Italian Parnassus, still were good enough of their kind. As an old man he had a passion for poetry, and some of us were allowed to hear long passages of a hendecasyllabic poem in which he celebrated his own life's work. Later, when I was his guest at Caprera, I heard him declaim from memory all the *Sepolcri* of Foscolo, and whole passages in French from Voltaire's *Zaïre*, and I recall that he knew many episodes of the *Iliad*, of Dante's *Divine Comedy*, and Tasso's *Gerusalemme Liberata*. One could add that for forty years he veritably

[4] Giuseppe Guerzoni, *Garibaldi: con documenti editi ed inediti*, Florence, 1882, Vol. I, 15–17, 211–13.

inundated Europe with his manifestos, appeals and letters (alas, that torrent of letters!), until the day arrived when the world saw him "in order to earn a livelihood" (a terrible phrase which ought to make us truly ashamed of ourselves) turn to writing novels. So doing, he added three volumes to that long list of things which history ought to forget about him.

Nevertheless, in order to read a maritime chart, to find your position at sea, to observe a barometer and keep a log-book, to sail your ship through the Pacific and the East Indies, all this betokens some serious education. To be able to write even second rate verse is something, especially when you remember that he occasionally produced passages of fierce and genuine harmony. To enjoy Ugo Foscolo, to understand Voltaire, to know something of Dante, Tasso and Homer, to put together even third-rate novels, to pen such a wealth of letters which, even though rough and sometimes bizarre, could sometimes show beneath their eccentricities and mistakes an occasional flower of wild beauty, to do all this (and to know as much as he did) he must have read and studied a good deal. . . .

There was one unfortunate defect in the Garibaldi who returned to Italy [in 1848], for although South America had been an excellent training ground as far as his military education was concerned, it was not, and could not possibly have been, a good school of politics. There he had found people of vehement passions, perpetual factions and regular revolutionary upheavals. It was a place where every *caudillo* at the head of a band of gauchos could aim at usurping dictatorial powers, only to be in his turn overturned by another *caudillo* more fortunate than he.

This was hardly the environment where a young man such as Garibaldi could form his political outlook and educate himself in the respect for law, in love of order, or learn a true idea of genuine liberty. Ingenuous, untutored though full of fantasy, his cast of mind was naturally molded as if in wax by the characteristics of a country which had offered him such hospitable refuge. It was a country whose brave inhabitants and picturesque countryside he greatly admired, and with these South American people he sealed an indissoluble pact of brotherhood on the battlefield itself. Inevitably this left its mark, and especially so in that it was the place where for the first time he heard, not surreptitiously, not in secret conspiracies as in Italy, but openly championed and openly defended by arms the words *fatherland, liberty,* and *independence.* These were the words which acquired sole dominion over his mind and became the chief religion of his heart.

Garibaldi thus lived half his life cheek by jowl with corsairs, soldiers, sailors and cattle ranchers, without any chance to refresh his memory about the virtues of a more civilized and cultured society. His own wild instincts, his habits as a sailor, his love of solitude and above all his overmastering desire for independence, these led him to find in the vast deserts of the pampas just what he had already discovered in the infinite spaces of the ocean. In this way he was led to admire, perhaps to envy, the life led by the wild inhabitants of the pampas. Can we wonder that in his eyes the *gaucho* came to represent the best type of free man? Can we wonder if he gradually learned to think, to act, even to dress like that section of the human family among whom he had grown to manhood? Nor should we be surprised that one day he brought back to Europe not only their ideas and beliefs, but also their personal habits and clothes.

The Garibaldi who came back to Italy in 1848 was thus a *gaucho*, even though modified by his previous links with Europe and purified by a high ideal of humanity. He was another José Artigas, but less vain and less obstinate—another Rivera, though more disinterested, more fortunate and more able. Time and the habits of civility would partially change him after 1848, but a *gaucho* he fundamentally remained all his life.

10

As a Soldier, Seen by Other Soldiers

Carlo Pisacane helped to organize the fighting at Milan, in 1848, and at Rome, in 1849. His criticism of Garibaldi's tactics at this early period must be taken seriously, especially as it is partly confirmed by criticisms of Emilio Dandolo (The Italian Volunteers and Lombard Rifle Brigade, London, 1851, *pp. 227–39*). *Garibaldi's "victories" at Luino and Morazzone against the Austrians in 1848, just like his success at Velletri in 1849 against the Neapolitans, were no doubt deliberately exaggerated, and properly so, in order to keep up the spirits of the heavily outnumbered revolutionary forces. Nevertheless, all three of these engagements can be defended as minor triumphs that owed something to Garibaldi's novel methods of warfare. Their contribution to morale, and to the* mystique *of national feeling, must have been considerable.*

Pisacane had been trained as a professional soldier in the regular Neapolitan army. He was accustomed to proper discipline and order in troops; he liked uniforms and a proper turn-out; and he did not approve of a commanding general giving orders to a corporal without going through the normal channels. But his criticism would have been more persuasive if he had shown a fairer appreciation of the tiny force at Garibaldi's disposal, of the methods of irregular warfare, and of the inescapable need on these occasions for improvisation.

COLONEL PISACANE CRITICIZES GARIBALDI AS A SOLDIER, 1850 [1]

General Garibaldi in Montevideo showed an unrivalled courage and gained great experience in commanding small maritime

[1] Carlo Pisacane, *Guerra combattuta in Italia negli anni 1848–1849* [written 1850–51], ed. Luigi Maino, Rome, 1906, pp. 143–47, 258–59, 270–73.

enterprises. Even when he came to command a few thousand soldiers on land, he preserved his reputation as a brave man who was generous and completely disinterested. No doubt these were more the virtues of a simple citizen than of a soldier, while the type of war he fought there, and the type of engagement he encountered, would not make one expect him to possess the knowledge and ability of a real general. It is indeed true that Garibaldi's maneuvres reveal no concept of strategy. His tactics are to make very long marches without any precisely calculated aim, and so doing he can tire his troops to no purpose. Once he reaches a strong defensive position, it is his practice to stop and wait for the enemy. I would say therefore that he is not even very good at partisan warfare, for this is a field where you need to be continually moving forward or backward. In battle he tends to use his men in small detachments, and hence he never obtains a decisive result. . . .

If Garibaldi [in August, 1848] had known his job he would have crossed the Po River with his column and proceeded south into Tuscany and the Roman states, the object being to start a popular uprising, to proclaim the republic and enroll an army. Instead he decided to stay in Lombardy. But here, too, it was open to him to throw his forces into the Valtelline where vast areas of mountain territory would have helped him keep his force intact. . . . Instead he let himself be confined in a tight position between Lake Maggiore and Lugano on the Swiss frontier, where he had no chance of breaking out to extend his movement. In a succession of useless marches, half of his men deserted, so that instead of providing a nucleus round which to recruit an army, his forces dwindled away. . . .

After five or six days of exhausting marches, his surviving troops were almost starving, and the town of Morazzone was far from happy when they arrived there. Fearful of revenge by the Austrians, the inhabitants of Morazzone were unwilling even to give them anything to eat, and only agreed toward nightfall and under the threat of force. Then, while these brave but badly led youths were eating, they were attacked by three battalions of the enemy, with one battery of guns and some cavalry. At once there was confusion. Garibaldi with a few men just managed to hold firm, but others fled in disorder from the gunfire into the surrounding fields. Later they re-formed and forced the Austrians to give way a little. But by that time Garibaldi had realized the deficiency of his plan. Seeing himself in danger of being surrounded, after four hours of fighting he ordered the retreat . . . and crossed into Switzerland. . . .

[On June 3, 1849, Garibaldi had a leading position in the defense
of Rome against the French.]

Hardly had his division reached the gate of St. Pancrazio, than
they threw themselves on the enemy. His Italian Legion and the
Lombard *bersaglieri* showed the greatest courage, and especially
these latter demonstrated discipline as well as courage. But Garibaldi, though immensely brave, did not sufficiently grasp the enemy
positions or give proper organization to the attack. Small confused
groups of ten and twenty men charged the enemy with the bayonet,
though luckily their courage was well supported by the artillery,
which fired 1,300 projectiles on this one day. The Corsini and Val-
entini palaces were taken and retaken more than once, and toward
evening the Lombard *bersaglieri* attacked for the last time and captured them yet again, but were so few in number that they were
driven back once more. Our soldiers were widely dispersed, and
there was not even a company of reserves to support them; so that
the enemy thus remained master of the field, even though it had
been a glorious day for both sides. . . .

A small skirmish at Luino and a defeat at Morazzone had meanwhile been magnified by the press into two splendid victories for
Garibaldi. They had been made out as a cleverer operation than
the more skillful campaign fought by the volunteers in the Tyrol,
and even better than the glorious battles of Pastrengo, Goito, Custoza, and Volta, etc. [fought by the regular troops of Piedmont].
The contemptible adulation of the press was due to ignorance and
not deliberate deceitfulness. Journalists imagined that they were
helping Italy by creating a legendary hero and substituting the
names of individuals for those principles which they had failed to
support effectively.

That was why Garibaldi, even before the republic was proclaimed at Rome, arrived there to find himself already famous, and
and so became the idol of a small group of excited youths looking
for an object on which to lavish their enthusiasm. These people
attributed to Garibaldi all the qualities of a great leader and statesman, as much as their fervid imaginations could contrive; and
these young men were in good faith; they were good Italians at
heart even though weak in the brain, and they thought that Italy
might be saved if only this man were proclaimed dictator.

A demonstration was therefore arranged, and it was hoped to
sweep people off their feet; but fortunately some honest citizens
spoke the truth to Garibaldi, explaining to him that the Constit-

uent Assembly was a more fitting place to decide the destinies of Rome, and that these few enthusiasts did not represent the real people. "General," said a friend, "go to make yourself Caesar on the Capitol if you wish, but first calculate the numbers of those who want you to act in this way, otherwise you may find your popularity gone." The demonstration in fact had no consequences, and the citizens remained silent.

A few days afterwards, the Assembly, elected by universal suffrage, proclaimed the Roman Republic. The executive authority and the Assembly then eagerly looked to see if they could discover some military talent, but found little of it available. Garibaldi was a soldier, as he was also an elected deputy, and he had already been acclaimed as a great military commander by the press, so that he should have been able to put his ideas into practice and tell them how the revolution could succeed. He would have encountered little opposition from either government or Assembly, for neither could have acted against public opinion, and his popularity conferred enormous prestige on any idea he might have chosen to put forward. As if by magic he found himself endowed with a reputation which any other person would have had to struggle to create. . . .

Garibaldi's sweet nature, accompanied as it was by genuine bravura, made him idolized by any who came near to him; but the further away you were from his direct personal influence, and the nearer you were to where ideas had to be put into practice, it was the heavy hand of his satellites which always made itself felt. Moreover the Italian Legion which he had organized, though made up of brave young men, had officers who knew nothing of military affairs and who affected to despise all which was regular, disciplined and traditional. It must also be said that the organization of this corps had nothing which was really new or republican about it. All orders emanated from the general in chief, and this conferred a kind of cult-aura upon him and gave him what amounted to a despotic power. Those brave young men were blind enough to think that they had more freedom if dependent on a single individual than on a properly constituted government which had popular support.

All this helps to explain why the regular soldiers were all the more unwilling to leave Rome [in July, 1849] when they learned that the expeditionary force was going to be under Garibaldi's command.

COLONEL GEORGE CADOGAN (BRITISH MILITARY ATTACHÉ)
TO LORD JOHN RUSSELL (BRITISH MINISTER FOR
FOREIGN AFFAIRS), OCTOBER 31, 1859 [2]

Although Garibaldi later showed at the Volturno that he could command large numbers of men over a wide field of fighting, his forte was with small units, where speed, quick improvisation, reckless effrontery, and high morale could compensate for untrained recruits and poor equipment. Everyone agreed that he was unique as a generator of enthusiasm and at inspiring his men with exceptional courage and confidence. Colonel Cadolini went so far as to call him a tactical genius. With typical sarcasm and condescension, Mussolini was to put it a different way: "fortunately for himself, Garibaldi was quite illiterate, or else he would have read Clausewitz on strategy and so lost his battles" (Galeazzo Ciano, 1937–1938 Diario, Rocca S. Casciano, 1948, p. 92).

No doubt, Garibaldi was fortunate in being matched with generals who knew nothing of his South-American style of fighting and were not prepared to learn; but he must also be given credit for seeing how this style could be most effectively adapted to suit a mountainous country such as Italy. It might seem quite absurd that his own Chief of Staff sometimes did not know his plans until the last moment; but, in fact, one of the few advantages he possessed over the far larger and better-trained Austrian army was this ability to change his mind at the last moment. Here was the secret of how he usually managed to force the pace and keep the initiative even when he was apparently in retreat.

A cordial reception on the part of General Garibaldi when I visited him at his own request at Rimini, gave me a fair opportunity of studying the character and peculiarities of this remarkable man, above all of verifying all I had heard of his unbounded popularity and of the immense influence he exercises especially on the populations of more central Italy and which is summed up in the

[2] *Le relazioni diplomatiche fra la Gran Bretagna e il Regno di Sardegna, 1848–1860*, ed. Giuseppe Giarrizzo, Rome, 1962, Vol. VII, 409–10. Transcripts of Crown-copyright records in the Public Record Office appear by permission of the Controller of H. M. Stationery Office.

appellation affixed to his name with the lower classes of "il padre dell'Italia."

I attach more importance to the simple circumstance of this appellation than it would apparently deserve, in so much as it points directly to the peculiar virtues and qualities that have earned for Garibaldi the position he now has with his countrymen and which greatly influence the probability of its duration.

Garibaldi was formerly known to Italy and to the world as a wild, daring and enthusiastic republican, barely distinguished by personal bravery and military aptitudes from the more corrupt elements of the Italian movement in 1848. To a comparatively few only perhaps at that time was he known for that which is now on the lips of everyone, a sincere and unselfish patriot and an honest man.

A parallel has not been inaptly drawn between Garibaldi and Washington; and in all that regards disinterested love of his country, want of personal ambition, earnestness of purpose and energy of execution, few comparisons in history could perhaps be more fortunate; their virtues and their cause were the same but not so their education and intellectual capacities—a fact that may not be found without its bearing on present circumstances.

Gentle and cautious in manner, slow, measured and correct in speech, one can hardly help at a first interview attributing to Garibaldi a higher order of education and refinement than has fallen to his share or than is consistent with what is known of his history, origin and experiences. On further acquaintance, however, it becomes evident that his educational acquirements are not great and that his views, although broad and honest, hardly ever rise above the level of trite and popular generalities. But for this very reason, perhaps, he exercises an influence on his hearers which a more cultivated intelligence might fail to have. Add to this a voice of singular charm and a manner that brings conviction with it as to the sincerity of the speech, and it can be easily imagined that it is no exaggeration to say he could make his followers go anywhere and do anything. I was myself a witness to all I describe on the occasion of a visit made by General Garibaldi to the outposts when he addressed a few words to the soldiers who crowded round the brigade headquarters with incessant *viva's* during the whole time of his stay. It would be impossible to do justice to the familiar and paternal, though not undignified, character of the few words thus spoken, or to the enthusiasm they produced. . . .

An utter indifference to his own wants, with boundless liberality to those of others, a simplicity of character, with almost childish illusions as to human nature which not even his hard experience of life has been able to destroy, all comes into the list of qualities attributed to him, and all I believe would be readily granted to exist by any one admitted as a spectator to the intimacy of his everyday life.

MARSHAL MAC MAHON: AN AFTER-DINNER CONVERSATION IN PARIS, MAY 24, 1860 [3]

"Garibaldi is a good sailor [said Admiral Bouet], probably a better sailor than general. His father was a Nice fisherman, and he passed the first twenty years of his life on the sea. I believe that he steered first for Tunis, and then ran up northward to Marsala."

"Cavour," said the Prince [Prince Jerome Napoleon], "took what he is not accustomed to do, a middle course. He should either have stopped Garibaldi or have given him five thousand men. He has thrown on himself and on my father-in-law [King Victor Emanuel] all the discredit, such as it is, of having favored the expedition. He would not have been more blamed and hated by the reactionaries if he had given it real aid."

"Garibaldi's popularity in Paris," said Bouet, "is enormous. All the portraits of him disappear as fast as they are published. Some of my servants were at a bourgeois wedding the other day—there were fifty or sixty guests. Nothing but Garibaldi was talked about; even the bride and bridegroom seemed to think of nothing else."

"I do not believe," said MacMahon [Marshal of France, and commander in the Lombard campaign of 1859], "that he will ever be a general. He wants comprehensiveness. He cannot foresee or provide for results distant in time and space. But he is an admirable "partisan." When he was in Italy with his four thousand men [in 1859], one of his spies told him that he had discovered, a couple of leagues off, an Austrian force of about three thousand men, who were not aware of his proximity, and could be surprised and cut off. The spy was a traitor. There were twelve thousand Austrians, and the spy had been sent to decoy Garibaldi into attacking them. With his usual impetuosity he fell into the trap, marched against the Austrians, and found, when he approached them, that they far out-

[3] Nassau William Senior, "Conversations with Prince Napoleon," *The Fortnightly Review*, London, 1879, Vol. XXXII, 172–73.

numbered him, and were prepared. Most men would have retreated, been followed, overtaken, and destroyed. He attacked the Austrians with such vigor that they thought that their spy must have deceived them, and that Garibaldi was in force. He drove them from their position and pursued them for a couple of miles, when they discovered the smallness of his numbers and turned back on him; his troops, active and unencumbered, saved themselves in the mountains."

"He will beat the Neapolitans," said the Prince, "more easily than he did the Austrians; and I do not believe that the Romans, even with Lamoricière, will stop him."

COMMANDER FORBES ON THE BATTLE OF MILAZZO, JULY, 1860 [4]

These red-shirted, ragged-looking scarecrows, under this far from prepossessing exterior, were endowed with many of those sterling qualities which have often enabled impromptu levies to triumph over more elaborate organizations. A musket or rifle, sixty rounds of ammunition, a water-bottle, and, for the most part, an empty haversack, and you have the *impedimenta* of a Garibaldian.

Of commissaries in gorgeous uniform there are none, yet of beef and bread there is an occasional supply—of discipline there is the mere shadow; all, however, are animated with unbounded confidence in their chiefs, and especially Garibaldi, who may be said to exercise an individual power over his followers wholly without parallel amongst modern commanders, who are too apt to lay influence on one side, and place their trust in fear. With this imaginative race, their faith in their chief almost amounts to a superstition: whatever he says, is—wherever he appears, victory follows as a matter of course. This feeling, combined with an utter contempt, and, with the Sicilians, an implacable hatred, for Neapolitans, has been the keystone of Garibaldi's successes, and of victories won in utter defiance of all martial tactics, as laid down by Jomini and other expositors of the rules of war. These writers appear to forget that every successful commander has created his own art of war, whilst the man of routine is invariably found pinned to precedent like some specimen beetle in a glass case. . . .

Garibaldi in person, as usual, was ever in the thickest of the fray,

[4] Sir Charles Forbes (Commander in the British navy), *The Campaign of Garibaldi in the Two Sicilies,* London, 1861, pp. 92–101, 118.

cigarette *en bouche,* and walking-stick in hand, cheering his guides and Genoese carbineers, his calm and benevolent features bearing their usual happy expression, as if he were on a day's excursion, rather than leading a death-struggle on which the fate of his country depended.

Strongly but symmetrically built, and of middle stature, this paladin of Italy is chiefly distinguished from his followers by his unassuming manner and aspect. Though dressed somewhat in sailor fashion, with a red shirt, grey trousers, wideawake, and loose bandana flowing over his shoulders, his appearance is scrupulously clean and neat, and his manner gentlemanly though genial. There is something most winning and honest in his address, and you are at once impressed with the conviction that you are face to face with a man whose word would be his bond, and upon whose guidance, either by sea or land, you would implicitly rely. No wonder, then, that his men advance again with such confidence where perhaps routine troops would have hesitated.

But it is hot work: Medici's horse has been killed under him; Cosenz has been hit in the neck; still the General leads his guides under Missori, and the Genoese carbineers, who ever behave admirably. Suddenly a three-gun battery opens on them with "mitraille" at twenty paces. In this murderous discharge Garibaldi was slightly hurt, Missori's horse killed, Major Breda killed, Statella alone left standing on foot with a few men. At the same time Malenchini, who had driven the advanced Neapolitans back on S. Marina, found it impossible to carry the hamlet—the road to it being completely swept by their battery; and the Garibaldians were again checked along the whole line. Garibaldi now gathered himself up for a fresh attack; and the reserve consisting of the English regiment having arrived, 150 men, with Major Wyndham, were sent to try and break through the line toward S. Marina; and Dunne, with the remainder, about 200 strong, was ordered by the General to advance and endeavor to carry the battery in flank; whilst Missori, Statella, and the remant of their men, attempted the same movement in the opposite direction.

Advancing under cover of a wall and ditch, Dunne led his men toward the battery, where he found, to his astonishment, Garibaldi before him, who joined in the fray. Dashing in after a momentary struggle with the infantry, the guns were carried, and in the act of being dragged off, when the Neapolitans opened out and made room for their cavalry to charge, and endeavor to retake them.

Dunne's men, unaccustomed to fire, behaved admirably, though driven out of the battery, where their colonel was knocked down and galloped over by the cavalry, not, however, until he had shot their leader. Dividing themselves on either side of the road, the Garibaldians placed their backs to the wall and prickly-pear bushes, and opened fire on the cavalry from either side. This was the struggle of the day, and very nearly cost Garibaldi his life, and with it the life of Italy. Afraid of advancing too far, and finding himself between two fires, the Neapolitan commander halted, and endeavored to return; but Garibaldi, Missori, Statella, and a handful of guides, barred the way. Summoned by the Neapolitan officer to surrender, the hero of Varese merely replied by springing at his horse's bridle and cutting down the owner. Three or four troopers seconded their officer; one of them Garibaldi wounded; Missori killed two others, and shot the horse of a third; Statella killed another; and this murderous struggle was concluded by Missori, who killed a third with the fourth barrel of his revolver. The remnant of the cavalry now charged back and escaped, leaving the guns in the hands of Garibaldi. . . .

Medici's men again bore the brunt of the fighting, and behaved right well in spite of their heavy losses. Some of the houses were gallantly contested; but the Neapolitans fought like beaten troops, and were evidently bent on gradually retiring to the castle, their retreat being covered by a heavy fire of shot and shell from that fortress, in spite of which the heroic Garibaldians gradually advanced from position to position, driving back the troops, until, about four o'clock, they worked their way up to the entrance of the castle. In the meantime some of Medici's men and Peard's company, following the Marina, on the eastern side of the peninsula, gained the heights to seaward of the castle, and established themselves near an old windmill, which completely overlooked the northern works of Milazzo, and rapidly rifled the garrison out of that quarter.

Nothing more could now be done for the want of heavy guns, as, from the height of the walls, and singularly strong natural position, the castle could not be escaladed. Barricades were thrown up in all the immediate approaches toward the town, in readiness to repel any sortie; and officers and men, alike worn out and weary, lay down on their posts for the night—Garibaldi, with his head on a saddle, under the portico of a church near the centre of the Marina. Their successes, however, had been dearly bought; no less than 750 Garibaldians were *hors de combat*. . . .

Garibaldi, when asked to write a bulletin after the battle by one of his generals, made a very characteristic reply: "No; if I write an account, I shall be compelled to say that some did better than others. You may write if you please; and the best thing you can say is, that the action commenced at daylight, and in the evening we had possession of the town. . . ."

There is a sort of intimate communion of mind between Garibaldi and the masses which is perfectly electrifying. They look up to him as a sort of link between themselves and the Deity.

LIEUTENANT-COLONEL CADOLINI ON THE CAMPAIGN IN CALABRIA, AUGUST, 1860 [5]

Our advance through Calabria was extremely rapid and in every way admirable. Some detachments on the very same day had to complete a march by land and also a further advance by sea. If you compare the date and the hour on which each unit began its advance, the operation looks a real miracle; and though we were continually in movement and sometimes short of provisions, we were never completely without food. . . .

Indeed the whole campaign of 1860 shows more than any previous operation Garibaldi's skill as a commander. For the first time he was in full command, heading a large army and without having to reckon with government interference. He now proved himself second to none in his intelligent application of the strategic doctrines of the Napoleonic school, adapting them to the special conditions in which he found himself, and to the fact that he was always facing forces much larger than his own.

Again and again I was able to observe that the dominant theme in Garibaldi's mind is how to unite all his forces together so as to attack the enemy at a decisive point with the greatest possible weight. . . . In this case he knew that dispersion of his forces was all the more to be reprehended in that these battles carried the whole future destinies of Italy, and one single defeat might have brought the national movement to a stop.

In such special conditions he had to adapt his plans to the fact that reinforcements from northern Italy used to arrive slowly and piecemeal, and this forced him to accept fairly long periods of waiting, which must have gone greatly against his impatient nature. He

[5] Senator G. Cadolini, *Memorie del risorgimento, dal 1848 al 1862,* Milan, 1911, pp. 427, 465–66.

showed real skill and firmness in the way he resisted the advice of politicians and the impetuous demand of his volunteers for action. He rather preferred to await the arrival of sufficient reinforcements before beginning his offensive. . . .

In Garibaldi's strategy one must first admire the firmness and prudence with which he knew how to wait; then the simplicity and speed with which he prepared his troops for action; then the speed of march by which he would concentrate his forces into a single mass, and the imperturbability with which he followed this by a sudden and vigorous advance.

11
The Critics: Left, Right, and Center

There were many reasons why Mazzini fell out with Garibaldi, some of them merely personal or casual, but some serious. Mazzini was a far more intelligent man and distrusted the other's easy ability to change his mind in the face of facts. He could stand neither Garibaldi's socialism nor Garibaldi's readiness to renounce republicanism as soon as an alliance with the Piedmontese monarchy seemed to offer the best chance of making Italy; nor could he appreciate Garibaldi's essential individualism. He did not understand the cautious calculation of expediency that made Garibaldi far better at exploiting rebellion once it was begun than starting one himself. Garibaldi, for his part, approved of neither Mazzini's personal authoritarianism and unreadiness to compromise —nor Mazzini's inability to admit that half a loaf was better than no bread at all—nor Mazzini's touching faith that a few intellectuals were representative of the Italian people. Mazzini was one of those strong, messianic believers who want to impose their religious as well as their political views on others, whereas Garibaldi was much more tolerant and easy-going, as well as more conscious of human frailty.

From another extreme position, and one which was equally authoritarian, Garibaldi had to meet the mindless opposition of the Irishmen who rioted repeatedly in Hyde Park to the war cry of "No Garibaldi! The Pope forever!" The Dublin Review *(London, 1864, Vol. III, 138) reviled him as "this man of violence and blood, this notorious pirate and filibuster, traitor and rebel, . . . the school-girl's corsair in a revolutionary dress." Archbishop Manning prophesied a judgment of God against a propagator of the "disgraceful principles of 1789," and preached a sermon against him that amongst other things maintained that "Italy has no more claim on Rome than on Dresden or Paris" (Henry Edward Manning,* Christ and Antichrist, *London, 1867, p. 9) .*

When Garibaldi, despite disagreement, had kind words for Mazzini, it was anti-clerical as well as clerical conservatives who were horrified, for Mazzini was quite unfairly thought to be an evil man and an assassin (Letter to Rendu, in L'Italie de 1847 à 1865, Correspondance politique de Massimo d'Azeglio, *Paris, 1867 p. 177). "He is a soldier of fortune," said Cavour of Garibaldi, "and behind his outward petulance there lies the profound dissimulation of a savage." (Una* silloge di lettere del risorgimento, 1839-1873, *ed. C. Bollea, Turin, 1919, p. 439.) "He is an animal," exclaimed Scialoia with contempt and even disgust; he is a person of "egregia be-stialità." (Carteggi di Cavour: Liberazione del Mezzogiorno, Vol. II, p. 379.)*

Such a remark betrays a certain amount of meanness, insensitivity, even foolishness; and it is not unimportant that most of Garibaldi's severest critics relied on hearsay rather than direct acquaintance. Some of what they said cut close to the bone. No one, certainly, could claim that he was a clever person, and sometimes he did not even seem sensible or clearheaded. Nevertheless an aristocratic critic, such as Azeglio, was too remote for complete fairness and accuracy.

A CRITICAL VIEW BY AZEGLIO, A CONSERVATIVE EX-PRIME MINISTER, 1864 [1]

I have always liked and admired Garibaldi. At the moment of his defeat in 1849, we were engaged in negotiating peace between Piedmont and Austria, and I instructed our negotiators to do what they could to see that his life was spared. Subsequently I procured him the offer of a government pension, which, though he refused it for himself, he accepted on behalf of his mother. I agree with you [this letter was to the director of the British Museum] that he is one of the finest characters whom God ever created. He loves his country, he is brave and warlike, basically honest, humane and generous, and has no desire at all for personal gain; moreover I agree that he rendered immense service in defeating the Bourbons

[1] Massimo d'Azeglio, July 25, 1864: *Lettere ad Antonio Panizzi,* ed. Luigi Fagan, Florence, 1880, pp. 479–83.

of Naples. In sum, for everything you say in his favor, I will say very much more.

Nevertheless I must also insist that no merit or service ever gives any citizen the right to place himself above the laws of his own country and violate them, especially when he goes on to justify such violation as perfectly proper and respectable. No one must be allowed to set himself up as a state within the state, or to treat with his sovereign as one Power toward another, or to outrage legally established authority in his own country. No single person can be allowed to appoint himself as a permanent judge of peace and war, or to generate a continual unrest which will expose his own country to expense, anxiety and danger. No one has the right to set his fellow citizens against each other in a civil war.

Our good Garibaldi has an open nature and lacks malice. I know he has been incited to his actions by rascals who need a braver leader than Mazzini would be. Hence they have made him drunk with incense and poured adulation on him such as would have turned the wits of a bronze horse, let alone a man like himself. But in a new state such as Italy today, exposed as we are to the sheer corruption and the almost irreconcilable internal differences inherited from our various *anciens régimes,* the primary need is to re-establish a public conscience, to assert the idea of law, of respect to the government, and of the sanctity of duty. In this matter of law, you yourself call us behindhand and say we should learn from the English. I don't absolutely deny this, but I must say that it is not entirely clear who should learn from whom.

After Aspromonte, the government of Rattazzi did me the honor of asking me and others to come to a cabinet meeting where the fate of Garibaldi was being discussed. My view was that he should be brought before the courts like any other citizen, but that after being condemned he should be allowed an immediate royal pardon. Unfortunately, since in the pockets of his red shirt he apparently had a certain piece of paper, etc., etc. [referring to a communication from either Rattazzi or the King which had authorized, or at least incited, Garibaldi to the disastrous expedition which led to Aspromonte], it was thought better to avoid the whole problem by proclaiming a general amnesty. This amnesty he rejected, arguing that he had just done what he had been forced to do, etc., etc.; and so the matter ended. . . .

Now let me come to this question of Garibaldi's visit to England. Obviously, as he had been preceded by a fantastic legend such as no one else has ever possessed, Garibaldi's arrival in London could hardly pass unobserved. Indeed I would have found it quite natural that he should be received, acclaimed and dined in the London clubs, and by everyone else including the Italians of London. But, that a man who claims to be always above the law, a man who is still wet with blood, responsible for the deaths of so many poor Italian soldiers, should be officially received by the government, by parliament, by ministers, by the heir to the throne, and given honors which no sovereign ever received—and that all the highest names in England should pay him homage—that is intolerable. Above all, you must consider that this is a person who has proclaimed himself a friend of Mazzini, that is to say a friend of the man who if he could do so would have all of us hanged, a man who publicly champions the morality of political assassination and has already let loose so many murderers in Europe. . . .

In Italy, on the other hand, Garibaldi's partisans have given him so much exaggerated praise that public opinion has now just about had enough. A great deal has been spoken about his disinterestedness: but if I had gained everything I had aimed to get, I too could be disinterested. It is the Italian government who has had to pay all the bills for him and his friends. You have no idea of the daily consumption of champagne when he toured through Pisa to Sarzana encouraging the formation of rifle clubs. His much-talked-about simplicity hardly squares with his fancy-dress outfit, itself a kind of charlatanism that does not go down too well in Italy. We had to watch his companions throwing themselves on titles, decorations and pensions just like coursing dogs on a hare. The officers of his volunteers managed to do much better than many brave and senior soldiers in the regular army, yet two-thirds of them then had to be dismissed by the councils of discipline either for misconduct or for ignorance of their job.

Another point to remember is that at the battle of Volturno and at Gaeta [in 1860], as everyone knows, Garibaldi would have been destroyed had it not been for the Piedmontese army. It is obvious now that, if we owe Naples to Garibaldi, it was General Cialdini who conquered the Marches and Umbria for Italy, and there are others too who have a similar claim on our gratitude. But in any case we cannot allow that such people should exploit this gratitude to make themselves the boss and play the tyrant.

I tell you all this because you live far away from Italy and cannot imagine how things look here and how people think from day to

2

day. But on this point I will finish, and just say that with Garibaldi, as with everyone else, one must praise him for what is good, blame him for what is bad, and above all not allow him to set an example of violating laws which we should regard as sacred.

A CRITICISM BY MAZZINI, 1867 [2]

I do hope that Garibaldi will not succeed in starting a movement [against Rome]. For at the moment it would probably be repressed, just as Rattazzi repressed that earlier expedition at Aspromonte; or else, if it succeeded, Rattazzi would take over control of the movement, and Rome would then find herself ruled by a small-time and immoral politician, by an intriguing lawyer who is as much corrupt himself as he is a corruptor of others. If Rome cannot be made the holy city of our Italian nation, it had better remain a ruin, for at least that would leave some hope for the future. One more year or less of slavery is nothing. What is vital is to secure that the flag of the Italian republic will one day fly on the Capitol hill, just as the flag of our religion of progress must one day fly over the Vatican!

Is this just a dream? I truly believe not. If I had time and the wherewithal I should be acting to make my idea into a fact. But I have neither. I have no money, and I have little time left to live. Somebody else will succeed. Garibaldi might do it if he were more intellectual. He loves Rome, but does not make this love a real *religion*. Please don't tell me that he is too honest to be a politician. He ought to be a real believer, but is not. He looks at the matter more from a *materialistic* than from a moral point of view, thinking more of the body of Italy than of its real soul. It is not in his nature to act otherwise. I don't accuse him, I just note this as a fact. Garibaldi is a brave person, noble, good, a man of integrity, and indeed he is unique; but there is *something lacking*. He does not measure up to our real needs.

THE VIEWS OF A JESUIT, AFTER GARIBALDI'S DEFEAT AT MENTANA, 1867 [3]

Garibaldi had his heart set on winning Rome from the Pope, and hence continued to declare a permanent state of

[2] Letter of August 5, 1867, to Caroline Phillipson, in *Scritti editi ed inediti di Giuseppe Mazzini*, ed. M. Menghini, Imola, 1940, edizione nazionale, Vol. LXXXV, 165. Reprinted with the permission of the publishers, Paolo Galeati—Imola.
[3] *La Civiltà Cattolica*, Rome, 1867, Vol. XII, 396–407; and 1868, Vol. II, 408–11.

open war on the papalists. This antagonized many conservatives who wanted something more subtle, and who were outraged that this lonely man in Caprera should be able to force the hand of the Italian government. Nevertheless, as General Cialdini discovered with surprised annoyance, in 1867 it was virtually impossible to form an administration in Italy that did not come to some kind of terms with him (Carteggio politico di Michelangelo Castelli, ed. L. Chiala, Turin, 1891, Vol. II, 249–50).

Rattazzi, once again Prime Minister in 1867, had learnt nothing from the bitter experience of Aspromonte, but again allowed arms to be transferred to Garibaldi with government connivance, in order to start an insurrection at Rome. A large number of volunteers were given a free train ride to the frontier, and allowed to cross from Italian territory into the Papal States. Then, Garibaldi easily evaded a half-hearted surveillance at Caprera, and joined them.

At this point, Rattazzi sent an envoy to Rome, in the expectation that the mere threat of Garibaldi's advance might have been enough to persuade the Pope to make terms. When this failed, a carefully meditated second-line plan was put into action. Rattazzi made a public announcement that he was driven irresistibly by public opinion, and had to occupy Rome with Italian troops. The reasons given were, firstly, the need to defend the Pope against Garibaldi's invasion, and, secondly, that the Roman population was alleged to be appealing for deliverance from papal rule.

This disingenuousness fooled no one, and at once the French sent troops to defend the temporal sovereignty of the Pope. Garibaldi's advance guard had by this point arrived within several miles of the gates of Rome, but the unexpected appearance of French soldiers then forced him to withdraw. Before he could reach Italy, however, his ragged and almost starving troops were caught and decisively beaten at Mentana. He then recrossed the frontier, to be arrested by the Italian government who wanted to divest itself of blame.

The whole episode had proved a disaster. Far from rising to deliver themselves from the Pope, the Romans had welcomed French help in defending papal sovereignty against the Italians. Rattazzi's government had once again behaved with cowardice: they first encouraged Garibaldi to act, and then left him in the lurch.

> But the killing of 600 Italian volunteers, as a French jour-
> nal was quick to point out (Revue Contemporaine, Paris,
> 1867, Vol. XCV, 169), caused such a shock in Italy that the
> end of the Pope's temporal power was rendered almost in-
> evitable sooner or later. Garibaldi was thus enabled to claim
> that his action had in this way been justified; and though his
> personal reputation seemed badly shaken by such a humili-
> ating defeat, it now seems that he emerged with far more
> credit than the King or the politicians. At the time, however,
> he was an easy target for the extreme Catholics.

The Italian government [in September, 1864] entered into a
solemn treaty obligation not to invade the small area of territory
round Rome which it had so far failed to snatch from papal authority. Even more, it undertook to defend this remaining portion of
papal sovereignty against any invasion by the revolutionaries. But
how has it kept these promises?

We have in fact seen bands of revolutionary volunteers organised
publicly in every city of Italy. Committees have been allowed everywhere to collect money and munitions for them. Officers have
been encouraged to leave the army in order to organise these volunteers. And, finally, thousands of them have been allowed to cross
the papal frontier at many different places. Secret orders were sent
to local authorities not to prevent enrollment. Some town councils
were permitted to help the revolutionaries with money, and the
National Guard gave them arms. Regular soldiers have even been
allowed to exchange their military uniform for the red shirt. Meanwhile a large Italian army gathered at the papal frontier, but not
to stop this aggression; their only object was to exploit any victory
won by the volunteers.

The Italian government proceeded by degrees along its iniqui-
tous course. First it allowed individual volunteers into papal territory, hoping that this would be enough to make the population
rebel and renew that same comedy which in 1860 let them take
over Umbria and the Marches. When the local population obviously showed no intention of responding to such an invitation,
and when these small bands of volunteers were in fact easily
defeated, then it allowed larger and better armed units to move
into papal territory. When even these were barred by the valor of
the papal troops, it then gave arms and men to Garibaldi himself
so that he could appear in person. This is the way that a

government which calls itself civilized carries out a solemn undertaking! . . .

No better moment could have been chosen for an insurrection to succeed. The French had been deceived by the lying promises of the Italian government and were delaying the embarkation of their troops for Rome. The small papal militia was mostly busy in the provinces, and on some days Rome itself was left with almost no garrison at all. . . . Yet the Romans remained loyal and defied the intrigues of the impious aggressor. Even more, they actively helped to keep order under the command of princes from the aristocratic families of Rome, forming many patrols and a unit which called itself the palatine guard. These groups kept watch and ward at night so as to give the militia some rest. All glory to these splendid citizens of Rome, and glory too to the papal government for knowing how to attract such affection and loyalty.

It would be hard to find sufficient praise for the small papal army of about eight thousand men, and hard to exaggerate the honor which they won for themselves and the Holy See. Not only did they have to defend the city of Rome itself against outside enemies and internal disturbances, but in small groups they had to guard a lengthy frontier against numerous bands of Garibaldian invaders. Yet they were victorious everywhere, and the difficulty was sometimes not so much to beat the enemy as to catch him as he fled. Often the Garibaldians ran away at the very first sight of our troops.

The valor of our small army will go down in history and is only to be explained by supernatural intervention. The Zouaves, the local papal troops, the Légion d'Antibes, were all equally superb, though as generous and brave men they all awarded the palm to each other. Such was their abnegation that often they had to march or fight for whole days without food and in heavy rain. Many had no bed to sleep in for three weeks on end, and had to be content with snatching an occasional nap in a haystack or on the bare ground. Their piety was exemplary. Officers and soldiers confessed and went to mass before fighting; and then, having made peace with God and been given celestial grace, they threw themselves like lions into the battle. Except for one small engagement at Monterotondo, this papal force always triumphed, for the consciences of the enemy were tormented by remorse and they were indelibly stamped with a papal anathema. . . .

Even at Monterotondo, moreover, this comic hero Garibaldi, with his two sons, finally sneaked off under cover of night to the safety of the nearby Italian frontier, leaving us victorious. His flight seems quite inexplicable. He had a superior force and well-trained soldiers; he possessed artillery, and was holding a fortified position on a hill which would have been hard for us to attack. Why then did you turn tail, O hero? Can you not see that your fear of defeat has ruined your reputation with your own side as well as ours? Surely it is better to die bravely than to run away like a coward. You yourself had given the watchword "Either Rome or death," and no one would have imagined that you had a third alternative up your sleeve—flight! You had boasted that you would make the papal mercenaries run away, but now it is obvious that you have done all the running. Among all the humiliations which God could bestow on you, this was the greatest, to make you run away from the papal soldiers. Poor Garibaldi! Until now he has been the hero of Marsala. Henceforward he will be the coward of Monterotondo. . . .

The revolutionaries had at first insisted that the population of the residual papal state was eager for rebellion and would rise on any promise of outside help. But this population, especially in Rome itself, has been completely loyal and devoted to the government. . . . The militia did not have a single deserter. Eager to fight, they supported a small group of regular Zouaves and scored the first success of the campaign at Bagnorea. The difficulty was rather to placate those whose repeated requests to be allowed to fight could not be granted. The papal government thus had this triple success, because of the political sense shown by its public functionaries, because of the devotion and loyalty of the population, and because of the heroic valor of our volunteer forces. . . .

Wherever Garibaldi goes he has been accustomed to be met with cheers, drums, trumpets, bells and frantic applause. Fashions of dressing *alla Garibaldi* have given work to tailors, and makers of hats and shoes. Cafés have been called after him. His sulky face was shown in shop windows, and his picture figured on the walls of taverns and public lavatories. Town councils called streets, squares and theaters by his name. The "democratic societies," almost all made up of foolish people led by sharp operators, likewise used his name and celebrated his birthday each year. The more respectable conspirators in parliament never tired of singing hymns to him, while cabinet ministers served as his acolytes and kings called him their friend. . . .

Not that he is entirely ill-equipped to play the roles assigned to him. On the contrary, he knows how to ride, how to fence, to shoot (and, even more, to use a dagger). He is equally at home in the masquerade of a triumphal entry, or in an undignified flight—whichever appears in his interest. He is quite content to renounce some grand honorific appointment made by the King, though he does not renounce that of being a spy for a foreign power [the United States] —and the evidence of a high official, repeated in a hundred newspapers, has credited him with this title.

Garibaldi knows how to speak like one of the people. He loves strange and vivid clothes. He lays down the law on politics and gives his views publicly on almost everything else. While he curses those who unfairly tax the poor, he sets himself on a level with the greatest in the land. He speaks with passion about the working classes and poses as a defender of the oppressed, claiming that he himself is a poor man and an enemy of the bosses. In his conversation he is brutally direct. To those who agree with him he is indulgent, and he is affable to the highway robbers who form his band. He is the enemy of all useless cruelty, yet he can be as fierce as a Turk in his idea of what constitutes justice and honesty. Though he can affect a fine sense of religion, it all boils down to cursing the Church and calling for the blood of the clergy. . . .

For some reason, men of judgment are more moved to laughter than admiration over this man. It is not our fault if mention of his name makes soldiers of any regular army burst out laughing. Just you try using it in front of senior officers of the Italian forces, for instance Cialdini, Lamarmora, Menabrea or even Admiral Persano; and watch them smile. Even his adversaries seem to have agreed among themselves never to be truly angry with him. A few months ago an eminent French politician, speaking to a group of illustrious catholics in Belgium had occasion to say that "when I speak of the enemies of Pope Pius IX, I do not of course refer to the person called General Garibaldi"; and I am sorry to say that this name, instead of arousing indignation, just occasioned some convulsive laughter. The French soldiers who fought against him at Monterotondo, witty as ever, found the right name for him—*Duke-take-to-your-heels.*

We too, it must be confessed, have also been tempted to laugh when studying this "legendary epoch from Montevideo to Marsala," as that legendary parliamentarian, Guerzoni, calls it; and it is all of a piece with subsequent events until, as today, he has decided to rest on his laurels. This valiant lion, this Achilles, this Hercules, this Mars, this Jove—the more you try to force him into

the light of day, the more he retreats into the shadows, the more he
melts before your very eyes. Finally he is no bigger than a puppet—
gross, bearded, red-shirted, made to dance by other people without
him ever perceiving the fact.

Certainly we will not deny him the kind of courage and success
that befit a bandit leader from the woods; but if you try to find in
him the qualities of a politician or a soldier, or even those of a
brave junior officer, even though you look with telescope and micro-
scope it would be wasted time: you look for the hero, but find just a
marionette. We in Italy all know those dolls made of painted rags
and sticks. The puppeteer can dress them as king or clown alternately; he can fit them out with a hump-back if he likes; he can
make their voice angry or insinuating, bitter or loving, happy or
discontented; he can bring them on to the stage when he wishes,
and then hang them up in his locker until the time comes to pack
up and move to a new place. Nothing is more easily manipulated
than a marionette, and no puppet is more obedient than Garibaldi.

BAKUNIN AND THE SOCIALIST INTERNATIONAL, 1869 [4]

*The leading European socialists never took very seriously
Garibaldi's claim to be one of them. For awhile, Karl Marx
and his followers had hoped to lure Garibaldi into sponsor-
ing their network of revolutionary societies; one of Marx's
friends, Johann Becker, went to visit at Caprera in 1861, and
later so did Ferdinand Lassalle, after writing to Marx for a
letter of introduction* (Nachgelassene Briefe und Schriften,
ed. G. Mayer, Stuttgart, 1921, Vol. III, 345, 383). *But their
aims were wildly different from Garibaldi's, and there was in
fact little to distinguish his brand of socialism from a gen-
eralized, humanitarian radicalism of the Left.*

*Quite simply, he was appalled by the excessive riches and
excessive poverty that could be found in Italy. It needed only
his mention of a progressive income tax for the* Civiltà
Cattolica *to call him a communist and the propagator of red
revolution; but he was of course far from being either.
Bakunin's comment was nearer the mark: "He is on our side
in day-to-day politics but is against our ideas. . . . Too old
and obstinate to change his beliefs, he is tied by them to the*

[4] Michel Bakounine, "Lettre adressée aux citoyens rédacteurs du Réveil à Paris,
October, 1869," *Oeuvres*, Paris, 1911, Vol. V, 289–92.

old world which we are out to destroy" (Nello Rosselli, Mazzini e Bakounine, 12 anni di movimento operaio in Italia, Turin, 1927, p. 319).

The partisans of Garibaldi and Mazzini still dream of revolution, but there are many fewer of them than there used to be, because the infection of utilitarianism and personal ambition has created havoc among the younger generation in Italy. The Garibaldians differ from the rest of the parliamentary Left in being at once more generous but less shrewd. Yet it is important to note that there are growing differences between them and the Mazzinians.

General Garibaldi's party has a fairly elastic composition. If it lacks character, that is because it has no firm principles. What keeps it together is a kind of personal cult and a more or less blind faith in the destiny of a single hero. If Garibaldi were to disappear, his party would disappear with him. Its political and social ideas are so indeterminate and confused that sometimes they hardly differ from those held by King Victor Emanuel or that luckless politician Rattazzi himself.

Some of Garibaldi's followers can now be found in official circles, in parliament and inside the administration. They include a great number of people whose political ideas and personal interests are far removed from any thought of revolution. Apart from this group there is another, now much diminished and still diminishing, which is more ardent and turbulent, consisting of youths who are out of work, and of others who feel uprooted. These are on the whole more bellicose; they are above all looking for adventure, or at least they are trying to find a career for themselves. Such people possess nothing so obvious as a policy. The Garibaldian party has always been this kind of mixture, and now it is more so than ever. . . .

A great fighter for Italian unity, a great believer in the power and greater glory of Italy, a faithful servant of the king, Garibaldi can hardly be thought of as a real revolutionary. If sometimes he has favored revolution, that was only out of impatience and anger. He is too jealous of the honor of his country not to have experienced moments of real indignation, especially when confronted with the shameful submission of the Italian government to the advice, or rather the orders, of that dangerous benefactor, the Emperor Louis Napoleon. He has in fact reached the point of rebellion whenever submission has resulted, as it sometimes has done, in a decision to postpone indefinitely the "great destinies of Italy."

Above all he rebelled against the renunciation of the conquest of Rome, the eternal city.

Garibaldi has now led his party into two terrible defeats at Aspromonte and Mentana. But it seems that he is so tied to his own past, so infatuated with his own ideas, that neither of these two disasters has convinced him of the dangers of allying with the monarchy.

GARIBALDI ARRIVES IN SOUTHERN FRANCE, 1870 [5]

In 1870, after Louis Napoleon had been defeated by Bismarck and succeeded by a republican government, Garibaldi volunteered to fight for France in the Franco-Prussian war. Despite the efforts of the Italian government to stop him, and of French conservatives whose feelings were outraged by his offer, Léon Gambetta gave him a separate command at Dijon, and here he undertook the last military campaign of his life as head of the Army of the Vosges.

He came at last, the commander, the most romantic hero of our century, the most famous human being on the planet, the leader most sure of living in the hearts of future generations, a living man whose legend is already as firmly implanted as that of Wallace or William Tell, whilst the severest historical critics of the future will be unable to deny either the reality of his exploits or the originality of his character. Who shall say that Garibaldi was not brave, disinterested, patient under suffering, a living Don Quixote, with all the fine and noble qualities with which Cervantes endowed his hero and just enough of his simplicity to be beloved for it? A living Don Quixote! I repeat in all earnestness and respect, and yet there is this difference between the two, that whereas Sancho's master tilted against windmills and effected no practical good, the Italian Quixote set lance in rest against a tyrannical dynasty and shattered it past all possibility of restoration. Afterwards it is true that he tilted against the temporal power of the Papacy and there came to grief, but if that adventure did not upset the windmill, it shook it, and the windmill has fallen since.

When this hero came amongst us and walked through the station to his one-horse carriage we saw his face very clearly in the gaslight. It was a pale, grave face, much more like that of a student and

[5] Philip Gilbert Hamerton, *Round my House, Notes of Rural Life in France in Peace and War,* London, 1876 (2nd ed.), pp. 388–95.

philosopher than a hero of great exploits. We cried *"Vive Garibaldi!"* with some energy, but he answered with a tone of extreme gravity and sadness *"Vive la République Française!"* We thought they might have given him a pair of horses and even perhaps a little glorification of torchlight and of music, but that simplicity harmonized well enough with his personal character and habits, and also with the serious anxieties of the time.

It is difficult for Protestants to realize the unaffected horror with which the clergy and religious corporations of an old French cathedral city must have heard on awakening one morning in November, 1870, that this Garibaldi, who at a distance was to them like a rock in the deep sea, or like Satan chained during the millennium, was now actually in the midst of them. . . .

Not only was the clerical sentiment strongly excited against Garibaldi, but even in minds which had not much of the *odium theologicum* there existed a very strong national antipathy. There is nothing that a nation hates, said one who has known many nations, like another nation. It was felt by many Frenchmen as a slight on their national pride that an Italian should presume to offer them any assistance in the hour of their distress; and as no French general would serve under Garibaldi, so in the public opinion of civilians there was a feeling that he was a presumptuous intruder, who felt that, because he had beaten a few miserable Neapolitans in a little enterprise that had become famous for the mere romance of it, he could conquer the great armies of Germany, before which so many French generals had been compelled to retreat in disaster.

GARIBALDI'S EXPULSION FROM THE FRENCH ASSEMBLY AT BORDEAUX, MARCH 8, 1871 [6]

The motion was put that Garibaldi's election at Oran should be annulled on the grounds that he was not a Frenchman. Tremendous applause came from the benches of the Right, and the Speaker asked if anyone wished to say anything before a vote was taken. At once Victor Hugo demanded to be heard, and in profound silence he then spoke. What he said was admirable, and put with a calm indignation if that is conceivable. It went more or less as follows:

France has passed through a terrible trial, whence she has emerged

[6] Victor Hugo, *Oeuvres Complètes: Actes et paroles depuis l'exil*, Paris, 1912, Vol. XXXIII, 416–17.

bleeding, vanquished, and left in the lurch by the rest of Europe. In the past France always espoused the cause of Europe, but no other Power or ruler had the courage to come to her aid on this occasion. Not a single state! Only one man came, but he was a Power in his own right. ("No! No!," *came furious cries from the Right.* "It is not true." *And insults were hurled at the name of Garibaldi.*)

I don't wish to be offensive, but I must say that, among all the French generals fighting in this war, Garibaldi alone did not suffer a defeat. (*This aroused an indescribable tempest. There were cries of* "Order! Order!")

I therefore demand that Garibaldi's election be approved. . . . (*It would be impossible to describe the tumult which ensued, until Victor Hugo finally gestured for silence.*)

"As your wishes are clear I will meet them, and even go further. For three weeks you have refused to let Garibaldi address you, and now I too am refused a hearing. I therefore resign from this assembly" (*Stupor and consternation on the Right*).

HIS DEPARTURE FROM MARSEILLES, FEBRUARY, 1871 [7]

It is finished—Garibaldi has quitted the soil of France. Who rejoices most, the Prussians or the peace-at-any-price Frenchmen? I think the entire population of Marseilles was on foot at dawn. Garibaldi's rooms have been full to suffocation ever since the doors were opened. I saw him at a very early hour; he was writing, signing, and rejoicing at the idea of seeing Caprera tomorrow. He gave me special commissions for the wounded Greeks, Spaniards, Italians. "We may meet again in fifteen days, you know," he said. "Yes, if I come to Caprera," I answered. At nine we entered the carriages, which had to proceed at a walking pace, so crowded were these wide streets of Marseilles. The National Guard and the soldiers tried to make a line round the carriage, but the ranks were broken continually. "There," cried a working man, "there goes our last hope!" "Ah! and glad enough they are," said another. Who *they* were he did not say. "Vive Garibaldi!" echoed from a thousand voices, blended with one "Vive la République!" "Vive la France Républicaine!" was Garibaldi's reply. As we neared the quay the carriages were separated. We descended for a triumphal procession; none of us would have cared for a crush; but the last moments were near— we felt him specially our own. As we went on board the orders were given to keep back the crowd; a wise precaution, as several times I thought the plank would have given way. He embraced us one by one, and of the tough red shirts—his own Genoese—not one can boast that he did not weep. Some sobbed aloud. Garibaldi's own eyes were full. We watched him from the pier as the steamer backed —then slowly steamed out of sight.

All is blank and tame, and void of interest. I never felt so forlorn. At Naples he left us in the same way, but then we were in Italy, and had our *rendezvous* in Rome. Now we are in France, foreigners and aliens, in the strictest sense of the word.

12

Casual Acquaintances

First impressions may not always be best, but they often contain a good deal of truth and sometimes can be deeply penetrating. Many people have left accounts of casual encounters with Garibaldi, and he greatly impressed many quite shrewd observers who were far removed from him in background and point of view.

No less a person than Gladstone thus thought Garibaldi a man of "admirable intelligence and good sense" (An Italian Englishman, Sir James Lacaita, ed. C. Lacaita, London, 1933, p. 151). *That hard-bitten officer, General Thaon Di Revel, was astonished, in 1867, to see the exalting, "electrifying" effect he had on ordinary folk* (Sette mesi al ministero, Milan, 1895, p. 71). *Giovanni Visconti Venosta, another conservative, commented, as did many others, on his voice—"the most beautiful I have ever heard"—and on the irresistible fascination he could exercise "even upon the most contrary." Watching him as he traveled through Lombardy, Visconti Venosta could hardly believe his eyes. Such was the effect on people that it was like watching "the head of a new religion" moving among the faithful* (Memoirs of Youth, 1847–1860, London, 1914, pp. 357, 378–79).

Two other short excerpts have a certain interest. The first is by Antonio Gallenga, who knew Garibaldi as a war correspondent in Italy:

Let any man propose anything "impossible" to Garibaldi, and he will attempt it. Propound to him any social theory utterly unintelligible and nonsensical, and he makes himself its advocate. But on the other hand talk reason to Garibaldi, make him aware of the error of his ways, appeal to his better nature, and you have your lion tamed, the most gentle, and forgiving, docile, and, what is more, sensible creature in the world (*Italy Revisited*, London, 1875, Vol. II, 292–3).

The other is by Karl Blind, an exile from Germany, who knew

him rather better: *"Of his natural intellectual aptitude, I con-*
fess, I hold a higher opinion than some of his democratic
compatriots would acknowledge. I am also convinced that
his so-called simplicity was far less than appearances might
seem to warrant" (The Contemporary Review, London, 1888,
Vol. LIII, 381).

EXILE IN THE UNITED STATES, 1850–51 [1]

Sad memories accompanied the champion of Italy to the New
World. A widowed husband, a baffled patriot, an exile from the
land for which he had so long toiled and suffered, his limbs racked
with chronic pains incident to prolonged exposure; his dearest comrades banished or executed—he seemed to have survived all that
makes life dear, except the distant prospect of giving that life to his
country. Yet his escape had been marvellous, and he must have felt
that he was preserved for a great end. His compatriots in New York,
among whom were several who had proved their attachment to the
cause he had so much at heart, and with them Avezzana and Foresti,
gave him a fraternal welcome. A home and friends awaited him in
a land of strangers; but, while he reciprocated earnestly the
affection thus manifested, he firmly maintained that spirit of independence so characteristic of his nature. No sooner was his health
partially restored than he engaged in regular and lucrative work,
assisting in a manufactory established by one of his countrymen;
and when his usual vigor returned, undertook the command of a
merchant-vessel.

It was during this period of his exile that we first saw Garibaldi
—when attending a meeting at the apartments of Felice Foresti, in
New York, held for the purpose of disposing of a fund which had
been contributed in aid of the Italian cause, before the unfortunate
termination of the revolution of 1848. Most of those present were
members of the committee through whose exertions the money had
been collected; and not a few were illustrious on account of their
sufferings or labors in behalf of Italy. Several projects were
discussed, it being at once determined to use the fund either to aid
the destitute or to promote, indirectly at least, the welfare of those
for whose benefit it was subscribed.

The silence and unpretending manner of one of the company,
seated in a corner of the room, attracted our attention. He was of

[1] *North American Review*, Boston, 1861, Vol. XCII (unsigned article, but no
doubt by Henry Theodore Tuckerman), 34–36.

medium height, with a frank and benign countenance, and yet a singular look of decision—one of those faces which combine modesty and candor with invincible will, the former qualities being indicated by an ingenuous expression of the mouth, and an unassuming air, and the latter by the compact brow and unwavering, concentrated glance. The breadth of the shoulders and depth of the chest, with a certain firm and commanding position of the head, gave the impression of power and authority; while the blandness, openness, and kindness of manner instantly won sympathy. As compared with the majority of Italians, we remarked in this man's bearing and aspect a grand simplicity and directness. He awoke confidence instantly. No one, with an insight of character as revealed by physiognomy, could fail to see in him the presence of one of Nature's noblemen. That his habits were thoroughly manly, his vocation one that had tasked the physical energies, his convictions individual and tenacious, his tone of feeling elevated, his spirit indomitable, his heart earnest, his purpose strong, and his nature disinterested, were impressions that gained upon the observer as by a kind of magnetic influence.

This estimate was confirmed when the moment came for him to utter his views, they were given with so little pretence and yet with so much weight and power of conviction. Without the superficial vivacity and the exaggerated manner so common to the Italian temperament, there yet was revealed a latent force and feeling all the more impressive from the contrast it afforded to the voluble and dramatic utterance of his countrymen. His calm manner, comparatively slow movement, and almost Saxon hair and beard, might have seemed characteristic of a northern rather than a southern European; yet his eye, voice, and air were essentially Italian. His nationality, however, was still more evident in the sudden, though subdued, emotion apparent in his language and expression, when speaking of or listening to what was said about his country. The passive man was then visibly stirred; the modest man became demonstrative; the silent man eloquent.

A TRIBUTE FROM THE FRENCH WRITER, GEORGE SAND, JULY, 1859 [2]

I was not surprised to find Garibaldi's portrait in the homes of the devout peasants who live in the mountains of the Velay and

[2] George Sand, *Garibaldi,* Paris, 1859, pp. 5, 13–15.

the Cévennes [in southern France]. This famous adventurer, who some fearful souls used to call a bandit, was here accorded a place among their pictures of the saints.

And why not? Why should he not stand with the patron saints of the poor? Many people in Italy even think of him as the founder of a new faith. What he says might almost have been said by one of the early Christians! His main doctrine is not a political thesis, nor does it spring from egoism or materialist calculation. His message was that, "I bring you danger, fatigue and even death. What I preach to you is the salvation of your souls, not the comforts of this present life. Rise then and follow me!" This is how he spoke to the peasants of Italy, and they rose in enthusiastic response to his appeal. Yet people say that the age of miracles is past! . . .

No doubt the king of Piedmont and M. Cavour saw that Garibaldi possessed something which, if not greater than, was at least different from that possessed by other heroic recruits who were enlisting to fight the national enemy. They saw him, and the people had already seen him, as a knight from the age of chivalry, as an apostle of liberation and a true initiator. They therefore gave him the part to play for which he was fitted by his prestige, by his unusual influence, by the magic of his inspiration, by his noble looks and the winning power of his patriotic faith. Charged to rouse the common people against Austria, and to proclaim the gospel of freedom even as he fought the enemy, he had an entirely new role to play in history. He was a revolutionary, but acting on behalf of a monarch, and he acted in this way deliberately, resolutely and loyally, without deceiving and without being deceived.

It is Garibaldi's inner thoughts and his moral achievement with which I am most impressed. His military exploits are known by everyone, and even in France this poetic figure, with all the added attraction of the unknown, has gained a hold on our hearts and imaginations. Nor is this surprising. Garibaldi resembles no one, and there is an aura of the mysterious about him which gives plenty of food for thought. Shallow minds may ascribe his prestige to youth or to his good looks; some would ascribe it to physical stength, or to his splendid voice; others to his physical stature and theatrical dress. But fortunately he dresses more soberly today, and yet his prestige nonetheless endures. He now wears a proper military uniform, and he is no longer in his first youth.

Garibaldi's features today have more in them of nobility and serenity than of beauty. He is neither monster nor brigand, but

rather a delicate and choice soul in whom it is the soul which commands and gives authority to the body. His soft voice is accompanied by a modest bearing and distinguished manners. He shows
great generosity and an immense good nature, though this is combined with an inflexible firmness of purpose and soundness of
judgment. He is essentially a leader, but he makes himself obeyed
by persuasion. He will govern men by their own consent alone. He
asserts no rights over others except through his word of honor,
given and received. This behavior has something about it of a
religious and visionary quality, and nothing similar is ever found
among regular troops. What we observe here is one of the strangest
manifestations of our age, and yet it appears in the midst of a war
which is based on calculations of expediency and the severest discipline.

Victory or death—here is the simple alternative in the mind of
this tiny army of partisans; and yet he has not once hindered or
interfered with the plans of the regular allied army. On the contrary, surrounded by his invincible heroes, bold as lions and
cunning as foxes, Garibaldi continues to pursue his own chosen
purpose in his own special way.

HENRY ADAMS: REPORT FROM PALERMO, JUNE 9, 1860 [3]

Garibaldi had apparently just finished his dinner, and was
sitting at a corner window talking with four or five visiters, gentlemen and ladies of Palermo. He rose as we came in, and came forward shaking hands with each of the party as we were introduced.
He had his plain red shirt on, precisely like a fireman, and no mark
of authority. His manner is, as you know of course, very kind and
off-hand, without being vulgar or demagogic. He talked with each
of us, and talked perfectly naturally; no stump oratory and no sham.
Just as an instance of his manner, there was one little action of his
that struck me. I was seated next him, and as the head of our party
remarked that I had come all the way from Naples in order to see
him, he turned round and took my hand, thanking me as if I had
done him a favor. This is the way he draws people. He talked
mostly in French, for his English is not very good. As for what he
said, it is of no particular interest to any one, at least as far as it was

[3] *The Boston Courier,* July 10, 1860, quoted in *The American Historical Review,* January, 1920, Vol. XXV, 247–48.

said to me. The others can report the conversation if they think it worth while to report what was not meant to be reported.

But this was only half the scene. At a round table in the middle of the room, a party of six or eight men were taking dinner. These were real heroes of romance. Two or three had the red shirts on; others were in civil costume; one had a dirty, faded, hussar jacket on; one was a priest in his black robes. They were eating and drinking without regard to us, and as if they were hungry. Especially the priest was punishing his dinner. He is a fine fellow, this priest, a slave to Garibaldi and a glorious specimen of the church militant. I have met him several times, rushing about the streets with a great black cross in his hands. He has a strange, restless face, all passion and impulse. The others were Garibaldi's famous captains—a fine set of heads, full of energy and action.

Here I was at last, then, face to face with one of the great events of our day. It was all perfect; there was Palermo, the insurgent Sicilian city, with its barricades, and its ruined streets with all the marks of war. There was that armed and howling mob in the square below, and the music of the national hymn, and the five revolutionary cannon. There were the guerilla captains who had risked their lives and fortunes for something that the worst envy could not call selfish. And there was the great Dictator, who, when your and my little hopes and ambitions shall have lain in our graves a few centuries with us, will still be honored as a hero, and perhaps half worshipped—who knows!—for a God.

And yet Heaven knows why he, of all men, has been selected for immortality. I, for one, think that Cavour is much the greater man of the two; but practically the future Italy will probably adore Garibaldi's memory, and only respect Cavour's.

As he sat there laughing and chattering and wagging his red grey beard, and puffing away at his cigar, it seemed to me that one might feel for him all the respect and admiration that his best friends ask, and yet at the same time enter a protest against fate.

As we came away he shook hands with us again, and took leave of us with the greatest kindness. As we made our way through the crowd across the square, we stopped a minute to take a last look at him. He was leaning on the railing of the balcony before his window, quietly smoking his cigar, and watching the restless, yelling crowd below. He seemed hardly to be conscious of the noise and confusion, and looked in his red shirt like the very essence and genius of revolution, as he is.

MME. MEURICOFFRE WRITES FROM NAPLES, AUGUST, 1860 [4]

I have seen to-day the face of Garibaldi; and now all the devotion of his friends is made as clear as day to me. You have only to look into his face, and you feel that there is, perhaps, the one man in the world in whose service you would, taking your heart in your hand, follow blindfold to death. I never altogether understood that feeling until his presence made it clear to me. It is the individual man and his personal influence that are so strong, but then it is the man exalted and sanctified, as it were, by his own single-minded devotion to and faith in a holy cause; and it is that which you see in his face, as though written in letters of light, and which carries on your thoughts from him as the man, to him as the type and representatives of his cause. One could love the cause without seeing him, but in seeing him you seem to be suddenly gifted with the power of seeing it as he sees it, and you love it better for his sake, while you wholly honor and admire him for its sake. I have often asked our marine officers who have seen him to describe him to me. They get on swimmingly about his shoulders, and chest, and head, and beard, and then they desire with all their might to describe his expression—but there they stop and gasp. Neither can I describe it to you. I can only say that it explains that devotion to the death, and, what is more, that faith in doing what the prudent world at large considers an impossibility, for his sake; it makes that feeling appear to you the simplest and most natural thing in the world.

A FRENCH NOVELIST DESCRIBES NAPLES AFTER GARIBALDI'S DEPARTURE, NOVEMBER, 1860 [5]

These Neapolitans have a lively imagination and love a spectacle. They go wild over words and gestures, and Garibaldi, with his public speeches just like in a kind of Greek democracy, was their ideal of a sovereign. He was friendly, accessible to everybody, and appreciative of applause and public demonstrations. At any hour he was ready to show himself on the balcony of a *palazzo,* or he would walk in the streets and along the sea-front, listening to the crowd and answering it. Even when in military encampment he allowed the poor to come and visit him. For the ignorant and un-

[4] Josephine Butler, *In Memoriam Harriet Meuricoffre,* London, 1901, pp. 50–51.
[5] Louise Colet, *L'Italie des Italiens,* Paris, 1863, Vol. III, 66–67.

fortunate he always had moving words inspired by charity and a fundamental belief in human equality. He conquered this town of Naples not so much by force as by sentiment and real human warmth.

When King Victor Emanuel subsequently arrived here, he, too, found a genuine welcome and enthusiasm. Even before his arrival he was already being worshipped as a symbol of Italy. But the Neapolitans are childlike and impressionable, and in their eyes a symbol must be clothed in forms which are attractive and captivating. And the truth is that Victor Emanuel in his public life has always despised charlatanism and theatrical touches. This simplicity has its own kind of grandeur, and to be sure it was enough to capture public opinion in northern and central Italy. But the South demands less seriousness and more verve. The King did not show himself sufficiently to the people when he came to Naples. He excited curiosity but failed to satisfy it. The pomp of kingship and the panoply of war were absent.

It was the same with the soldiers of the northern army, for they produced just the same impression on people. Duty and discipline came first with them, and they hardly mixed at all with ordinary citizens. And soon these brave soldiers, who came as liberators just like the Garibaldians, were being reproached for their aloofness and for behaving as though they had conquered Naples. Even their uniform was displeasing, as it recalled too much that of the Bourbon army, whereas the varied and picturesque—even theatrical—dress of the volunteers had enchanted everyone.

After Garibaldi's departure, a fair number of his disbanded volunteers were left behind at Naples, uncertain whether they were going to be incorporated into the regular army, or if they would have to return home. They had nothing to do. All day long they could be seen in the streets and cafés, and the citizens always took their part if they quarrelled with the Piedmontese soldiers. Many different types of grievance were now blamed upon the regular government. The Bourbons still held out in Gaeta, and this was one fact among many which antagonized public opinion in Naples. People felt sure that if only Garibaldi had remained he would have finally defeated King Francesco, although on this point their attitude was short-sighted and unjust. . . .

But so long as Garibaldi was in Naples, no opposition had dared show itself, for the rapidity of events had left all opponents of the revolution quite powerless before him. From this fact grew up a

popular belief that Garibaldi, in leaving Naples, had taken with
him the peace and prosperity of the kingdom. The whole town was
afflicted by a profound sadness which no observer could fail to notice. Almost at once the singing and the patriotic shouting were
stilled. No longer were there torchlight processions, no more did
joyful groups carry flags and cry their *vivas*. As a poet, I must confess that I shared this general feeling. The Naples of Victor Emanuel had none of the charm for me possessed by the Naples of Garibaldi. One no longer felt the gaiety, the expansiveness and the
excitement which had affected the whole people after their liberation.

JOHN MORLEY AND WILLIAM EWART GLADSTONE ON GARIBALDI'S VISIT TO ENGLAND IN 1864 [6]

London has seldom beheld a spectacle more extraordinary or
more moving. The hero in the red shirt and blue-grey cloak long
associated in the popular mind with so many thrilling stories of
which they had been told, drove from the railway at Vauxhall to
Stafford House, the noblest of the private palaces of the capital,
amid vast continuous multitudes, blocking roadways, filling windows, lining every parapet and roof with eager gazers. For five hours
Garibaldi passed on amid tumultuous waves of passionate curiosity,
delight, enthusiasm. And this more than regal entry was the arrival
not of some loved prince or triumphant captain of our own, but of
a foreigner and the deliverer of a foreign people. Some were drawn
by his daring as a fighter, and by the picturesque figure as of a
hero of antique mould; many by sight of the sworn foe of Giant
Pope; but what fired the hearts of most was the thought of him as
the soldier who bore the sword for human freedom. The western
world was in one of its generous moments. In those days there were
idealists; democracy was conscious of common interests and common brotherhood; a liberal Europe was then a force and not a
dream.

"We who then saw Garibaldi for the first time," Mr. Gladstone
said nearly twenty years after,

> can many of us never forget the marvellous effect produced upon all
> minds by the simple nobility of his demeanor, by his manners and

[6] John Morley, *The Life of William Ewart Gladstone*, London, 1903, Vol. II, 109. Reprinted with the permission of Macmillan & Co. Ltd.

his acts. Besides his splendid integrity, and his wide and universal sympathies, besides that seductive simplicity of manner which never departed from him, and that inborn and native grace which seemed to attend all his actions, I would almost select from every other quality this, which was in apparent contrast but real harmony in Garibaldi—the union of the most profound and tender humanity with his fiery valor.

He once described the Italian chief to me as "one of the finest combinations of profound and unalterable simplicity with self-consciousness and self-possession."

13
Friends and Disciples

GIUSEPPE BANDI, ONE OF THE "THOUSAND"[1]

I used to recall the saying about no man being great in the eyes of his valet, so I determined to make a close study of Garibaldi in the intimacy of his own home. This extraordinary person aroused such admiration as he rode with his troops into battle surrounded by all the aura of heroism and victory, but I wanted to compare this public figure with the same man who, once he had laid down his arms and his uniform, was seen very differently through the eyes of his friends.

At the period I am speaking about [the middle 1860's], Garibaldi's age was nearer sixty than fifty. Others who had known him during those first adventurous years in South America often told me that his nature had not greatly altered since then. They had always known him tranquil in the moments of greatest danger. He had always been kind, always temperate in good fortune and even-tempered in bad. Many other men have equalled him in vigor and faced death with equal courage, but rarely can anyone have been so serene in danger and so in charge of himself. One could say without fear of contradiction that danger and difficulties simply made him calmer, more clear-sighted, more judicious. The ability to take sudden decisions and then act on them with lightning speed were among his other more noteworthy characteristics. . . .

Born with the instincts of a soldier, Garibaldi took real pleasure in risky and venturesome enterprises. He liked to feel free to act on his own, just as he liked to feel he could rely on blind obedience, simply because he was so supremely confident in his own good luck and his skill in planning and execution. He did not often ask advice, and disliked being given it unasked. He loved liberty and it was what he fought for; yet to meet a real emergency he advocated giving dictatorial powers to a single individual. Some said he had acquired this attitude from observing the small republican dictator-

<hr>

[1] Giuseppe Bandi, *I Mille: da Genova a Capua*, Florence, 1903, pp. 342–51.

ships in southern America, but I would rather say that he had dictatorship in his blood; and I would add that the effectiveness and rightness of dictatorial methods became ever more obvious to him because of the kind of enterprise in which he found himself, where the secret of victory lay in speed, single-minded action, blind confidence in and admiration for a single man.

One thing which did a great deal of harm to Giuseppe Garibaldi was his habit of thinking all men honest, and his assumption that everyone was as selfless and devoted to their country as he was. . . . He preferred people of few words, and had a strong dislike of those who never stopped talking. He liked people to speak only when they had something to say, and yet he took no excuses from anyone who did not understand immediately what he said. Woe to those who made him repeat an order or who failed to carry it out precisely. Even his glance had to be obeyed! Yet we all looked on him more as a father than as a soldier or dictator. Merely to see him smile conveyed an idea of how good, how patient and modest, how full of compassion and genuine affection he was to those who were fond of him. . . . Above all he disliked people who were overbearing and proud, while what he chiefly valued in others was a feeling of personal dignity, even if excessive. Among foreigners, he preferred North Americans and Englishmen. . . .

He disliked priests, but his essentially gentle soul would never have allowed any less than courteous word to fall from his lips if a priest were present. This was why some priests, even those who had been told that he was the devil incarnate, learnt to admire and bless him after a personal encounter, and would protest that they had been deceived by those who called him a firebrand out of hell; this ferocious fanatic suddenly appeared to them as one of the most benevolent, courteous, even wise of men.

Garibaldi's education had been restricted, but he had a natural wit; he had read and travelled a good deal, so that he could talk agreeably and by no means at a disadvantage with people who were more sophisticated and learned. . . .

He never had a very precise idea of the state, or of the rights and duties of citizens with regard to the state, for he had grown up in countries where revolution was perpetual and everyone lived in an almost permanent state of war. Nor did he ever quite allow for the pressures under which statesmen must work in relation to other countries whose interests might be very different. There was no difference in his eyes between attacking an enemy battery and attacking the point of view of a more or less friendly government. He had little use for what others would call expediency, or even for international law. Differences of national interest between neighboring states had in his eyes no greater validity than any other kind of obstacle which might yield to a bold, frontal assault. His ultimate criterion, indeed his only criterion, was the goodness of his cause and the strength of his own right arm.

The happy outcome of his extremely audacious Sicilian enterprise in 1860 made him think it proper, even necessary, to force the hand of a pusillanimous government and assert his own idea of what was good for the welfare and glory of his country. Not once did Giuseppe Garibaldi doubt for a moment that he could go on to do against Austria and against the Pope what he had already done so successfully against the Bourbons of Naples; nor did he stop to think that action on his part might result in diminishing the authority of the king. . . .

Among the victories which he used to recall with particular pleasure was that of April 30, 1849, when he made the French soldiers take to their heels. More than anything else he hated the arrogance of the French, and above all he hated their Emperor, Louis Napoleon. Indeed his main reason for disliking the French was the fact that for so long they tolerated the imperial tyranny. For him this was unpardonable; and it also explains why, no sooner had the Napoleonic government fallen [in 1870], he volunteered to serve France with "what still remains of me."

It is said that Giovanni delle Bande Nere when on the point of death was still afflicted by the thought that cowards existed in the world. Garibaldi likewise never excused cowardice. Nor did he ever forgive those who remained supine under bad governments. That is why people used to call him the "knight errant of liberty." If only he had been given the qualities of perpetual youth, he would have gone on roaming the world in search of tyrants to fight and slaves to liberate. His ideal world was peopled by men who worked hard and honestly, and who had no use for priests or policemen. He derided diplomats and despised lawyers. Nor could he ever quite understand why the mayor of a town could not exercise his paternal government without being supported by police and prefects.

He believed in God—to the extent that he thought there was a wise providence and a beneficent force ruling in the world—though he did not understand the need for organized religion. Of all the practical arts it was agriculture which he held in highest esteem.

He loved old Italian music. Among poets he preferred Tasso and Ugo Foscolo. So much for those malevolent critics who made out this man to be a rough sailor, a brutal soldier of fortune, the enemy of God and man, with nothing of nobility about him!

JESSIE WHITE MARIO, ON GARIBALDI'S WOUND AFTER ASPROMONTE [2]

Meanwhile the General's health improved visibly, the inflammation and the swelling abated, although the agony, borne with a fortitude and serenity never surpassed, was sometimes terrible to behold. At last [after several months of ineffective probing by some twenty surgeons] Professor Zanetti, the great Tuscan surgeon, enlarging the orifice of the wound by inserting cotton-wool steeped in gum, felt prepared to make an attempt to extract the ball. Garibaldi held my hand during the whole of the operation, and as soon as the forceps entered the aperture he exclaimed: "Per Dio! c'e!" (By God, it's there). A few seconds later Zanetti produced the sharpshooter's bullet, which, striking first against a boulder, thence rebounding into the ankle, had assumed the perfect form of a cap of liberty, the point, deflected by concussion with the rock, forming the tassel.

It was a supreme moment of emotion when Zanetti held it up to view. Garibaldi embraced the surgeon, then all of us: the news spread—spread like magic, and rejoicing was universal. Sheets and bandages, stained with the blood of the martyr of Aspromonte, were eagerly sought for, and torn to ribbons for distribution, to be treasured as sacred relics. Menotti, the General's son, kept the bullet, refusing to part with it, though an Englishman offered a fabulous sum for its possession. Never did I pen such a joyful telegram as the one announcing to England that the ball had been at last extracted and that the General was "doing well."

Lady Palmerston sent him a perfect invalid bed, which could be placed at any angle for the patient's comfort, and on it Garibaldi slept; on it he was moved from Pisa to Leghorn, and thence by steamer to Caprera. Never was a gift so welcome, or so much appreciated; never was a gift so conducive to repose and the alleviation of pain. Though all danger had passed, excruciating pain was still suffered by the hero, every movement being agony because of

[2] Jessie White Mario, *The Birth of Modern Italy*, ed. Duke Litta–Visconti–Arese, London, 1909, pp. 329–30.

the arthritic complications; and never was suffering borne with such angelic patience, such care to avoid giving trouble, and such gratitude for the services that all were proud and thankful to render.

FRANCESCO CRISPI, HIS FORMER SECRETARY

This is the century of the poor, the century of the common man, and no one better than Garibaldi foresaw this fact and championed the cause of their redemption. Yet those socialists were in error who persuaded him to attend their international congresses and who used his name in order to validate their socialist theories. What one can truthfully admit is that he deeply felt in his own person the sufferings of the working man. He understood both the tyranny of the middle classes and the world of strikes. He had a heartfelt desire to reconcile the interest of those who work with that of those who profit from their work. He admired the peasant and the artisan; he honored sacrifice, in the same way as he honored the sacrifices made by his men on the field of battle.

I remember when in 1863 brigandage was such a problem throughout the Neapolitan provinces, and parliament was discussing special laws to eradicate it. Garibaldi put the blame squarely on the government and the possessing classes. His heart was broken at the news of the massacres and all the blood spilt. When he was told of these unfortunate people who attacked and burned farmhouses, slaughtered cattle, burned down woods and harvests, his answer was that this was fundamentally a social question which could not be solved by force and punishment. A friend one day told him that the brigands, when condemned by summary courts to execution, faced death without fear; and he exclaimed, "What a miserable waste of courage! If only these men had not been misled into taking up a life of crime, they would have been brave soldiers in their country's cause!" . . .

The word "dictator" has been used, and I hope I will be allowed to explain what this meant to Garibaldi. . . . It was as a dictator that Garibaldi ruled Naples and Sicily [in 1860 when Crispi had been his political secretary], and it was this dictatorship which made possible the unification of Italy. Nor let anybody say that this one man, even with so much authority, was the enemy of personal freedom. Though he had no parliamentary assembly to share the responsibility of government, Garibaldi as a politician made a genuine attempt to interpret public opinion. No one could have called his a military regime, because there was no sign of tyranny or rule by the sword. He was accessible to everyone, poor or rich, plebs or bourgeois. He introduced no law which limited the freedom of the press or freedom of assembly. In all his time in Sicily only three death sentences were passed: one scoundrel was shot because under cover of the war he sacked and burned several villages near Palermo, and two others were executed in the province of Trapani when found guilty of pillage and murder.

Garibaldi experienced no difficulty in exercising political power. The Bourbon army in June 1860 had scarcely left Palermo before everything returned to normal: taxes were collected without difficulty, trade picked up, and citizens returned to their usual occupations. What chiefly astonished men of affairs was that payment of interest on government securities was at once resumed by the new government and thereafter continued regularly. Sicilians remembered all too well what had happened under parliamentary government in their former revolution of 1848; they recalled the disorders, the financial and political difficulties of that earlier time, and could hardly imagine how Garibaldi now kept so much order with so much liberty. This was a dictatorship with all the benefits and none of the vices of dictatorship. It witnessed the harmonization of unlimited executive authority with the wishes of public opinion. The sovereignty of the nation was thus established without violence, and without being led astray by violent passions.[3]

Garibaldi was a parliamentary deputy in name alone, and he would have been wise to have kept away from parliament altogether. On one occasion he came to Turin [in April, 1861] and suffered a major parliamentary defeat at the hands of Cavour. A second time he came [March, 1862] in order to give his blessing to the government of Rattazzi and Depretis, who shortly afterwards rewarded him for his pains with the bullet of Aspromonte. If he had remained a soldier, he would have stayed at Caprera, and by now he would have been greater and more invincible than ever. The gods have not bestowed on Garibaldi the brains of a Cromwell, nor the ambition of a Napoleon. He is a real captain of the people, a tribune of the plebs. His arena of action is not parliament. Where he can exert his influence is rather in the public streets, the marketplace, and the battlefield.[4]

[3] *Nuova Antologia di scienze, lettere ed arti,* Rome, 1882, June, Vol. LXIII, iv–xii; obituary of Garibaldi by Francesco Crispi (Prime Minister 1887–1891).

[4] Letter by Francesco Crispi, January 7, 1864, ed. G. Pipitone-Federico, *L'anima di Francesco Crispi,* Palermo, 1910, pp. 35–36.

14
Writers

It is at first sight surprising that Garibaldi wrote so much, for he was essentially a man of action, and Italian was not exactly his native language. Though he had read a good deal, he was mainly self-taught, and his feeling for literature, though genuine, was extremely superficial. Carlo Cattaneo, that polymath scholar who shared few of his views, once said that Garibaldi expressed himself very well just because he said what he meant, simply and directly, never affecting sentiments or a style that did not come naturally (Scritti politici ed epistolario 1849–1863, ed. Gabriele Rosa, Florence, 1894, Vol. II, 299). Most people, however, thought, that his reputation would have gained had he written much less.

GARIBALDI THE POET, 1868 [1]

The *Star* has published a poem of Garibaldi's, "Garibaldi's Answer to Victor Hugo, transmitted and done into English by an Oxford Graduate." It shows decisively that Garibaldi has no common command of poetical rhetoric, some of which (as translated by the Oxford graduate at least) is exceedingly keen and brilliant. Take this, for instance, in apology for accepting Victor Emanuel after dethroning Bomba [the King of Naples]:

> To spare the Italy we loved this strain
> Of the old agony borne all again;
> We drove the Bourbon out and took that other,
> Dethroned a corpse, and set up its sick brother!

The poem is long, full of not so much the enthusiasm as the fanaticism of humanity, and entirely in Garibaldi's finest Shelleyan

[1] *The Spectator,* London, January 18, 1868, p. 63.

strain. There is one of his noble magnanimous touches in it—we mean the italicized words [italicized not by Garibaldi] on Louis Napoleon—

> Warned off from Mexico—foiled at Berlin—
> He slew my lads—my Roman boys! to 'win
> Prestige.' He won it. Ah! good Friend! thy verse
> Thunders the judgment of a righteous curse
> On those soiled laurel leaves. But let him be,
> He does the things he must! Wait thou and see!
> A little while his shameless scheme prevails,
> A little while, and God's long-suffering fails.
> And when he ends, *and we may pity him,*
> The dawn will break on Europe dead and dim;
> The dawn of brotherhood, and love, and peace,
> The light of a new time, when there shall cease
> This clang of armies over Christian lands;
> And nations, tearing off their Lazarus-bands,
> Shall rise—see face to face—and sadly say,
> "*Why* were we foes? why did we serve—and slay?"

Can anything resemble more closely in tone the spirit of Shelley's *Hellas?*

A REVIEW OF THE ENGLISH TRANSLATION OF
THE RULE OF THE MONK [2]

The title and the author of this book are calculated to excite a certain amount of curiosity. Most people will be amused at making acquaintance with General Garibaldi in the new character of a literary gentleman, and will be glad to hear his remarks about Rome, though it may be that they will anticipate less new light upon the Eternal City than upon the peculiarities of the General. The anonymous writer of a preface does what he can to heighten our curiosity. He is careful indeed to provide against adverse criticism by assuring us that "the deficiencies of the work are due rather to the translation than to the original"; but he adds that "the vigor and charm of the great Liberator's Italian are such as to show that he might have rivalled Alfieri or Manzoni, if he had not pre-

[2] *The Saturday Review,* London, March 5, 1870, Vol. XXIX, 321–22.

ferred to emulate the Gracchi or the Rienzi." Further, he is kind
enough to inform us that the narrative is "idyllic in the pastoral
scenes, tender and poetic in the domestic passages, Metastasio-like
in some of its episodes, and terribly earnest in its denunciations";
and if we were inclined to save ourselves the trouble of criticism,
we might be content to appropriate these words, omitting the marks
of quotation, and give them as our own judgment. Of course the
translator ought to know best a work over which he has taken so
much pains, and we will therefore give the General credit for an in-
definite amount of graceful language, the fine essence of which has
unavoidably disappeared from the English version. . . .

The following statements will, we hope, convey a tolerably accurate impression of the General's opinions about modern Rome.
Rome, as we know, is a city governed by priests. Now the General
"hates the priesthood as a lying and mischievous institution,"
though he is ready to welcome them to a nobler vocation when
they have divested themselves of their "malignity and buffoonery."
Meanwhile he regards them as "assassins of the soul," and therefore as more culpable than assassins of the body. A priest knows
himself to be an impostor, unless he is a fool; and generally leads
a life of the grossest sensuality whilst deceiving the people into the
belief that he is a virtuous ascetic.

It is easy to imagine what a priest must be when exalted to positions of power. Let us take, for example, Cardinal Procopio, the
Pope's favourite. Procopio once upon a time deceived a beautiful
girl, lodged her in his palace till the birth of a child, and then had
the child murdered, and turned the mother out upon the world in
a state of insanity. This was only one specimen of a long series of
evil deeds. Finally, by acts of the basest treachery, he gets another
still more beautiful girl into the same sink of iniquity, and at a
critical moment, when she is struggling with him and two of his
degraded myrmidons, three patriots, each of whom is also of ex-
quisite beauty, incredible courage, and most unblameable character
(qualities which belong to all true Italian patriots), surprise the
villains, gag them, and save their victim. Next morning the Roman
populace has the pleasant spectacle of the Cardinal and his two
minions dead and suspended by the neck from the windows of the
palace.

It is not often, however, that such condign punishment is in-
flicted upon evildoers in high places. As a rule, they carry on their
infernal tyranny with great satisfaction to themselves. They have

servants—generally priests—who are ready to go about committing murder and other atrocities on the slightest hint of their superiors. Thus, for example, a widow is left dangerously ill with a princely fortune and a small boy. A priest is told off to frighten her with fears of hell until she has left the whole of her property to the Church. Unluckily she shows symptoms of returning health. The priest accordingly goes to her house, and, assisted by a nun whom he has sent to her as a nurse, opens her mouth, pours a deadly fluid down her throat, and lets her head fall heavily back on the pillows, while a complacent smile spreads itself over his diabolical features as, after one gasp, her jaw falls. The priests, moreover, have chambers of torture in their palaces, of which they know how to make good use either upon patriots or, in case of need, upon their own wretched servants. "Bring the girl to me," exclaims Pro-copio to his menial, "or the palace cellars shall hear thee squeak thy self-praise to the tune of the cord or the pincers"; and we are assured that this was no vain threat, but that, incredible as it may appear to outsiders, tortures too horrible to describe take place daily in the Rome of the present day. . . .

We have perhaps gone far enough to explain the nature of the blessings enjoyed under the "rule of the monk." If a tenth part of the General's statements be true, most of the present rulers of Rome deserve summary execution or imprisonment for life. We will not attempt to describe the admirable race of beings who oppose their devilish machinations. Every Roman patriot is the quintessence of all that is most admirable in human nature. Elaborate plots are constantly going forwards in spite of the watchfulness of the po-lice, and when the conspirators are discovered and surrounded by overwhelming numbers, all they have to do is to throw themselves courageously upon the base mercenaries, who instantaneously dis-perse in panic from before a tenth of their number. Occasionally the patriots have to take to the woods and live with certain virtuous brigands, where the "idyllic scenes" described by the translator take place. The arcadian innocence of the persons concerned may be estimated by the fact that the marriage ceremony in an interesting case consists chiefly in an English heroine joining the hands of the contracting parties and pronouncing them to be man and wife. This "solemn act of wedlock," we are assured, is "none the less solemn nor binding" for being so celebrated. Attacks from the wretched set of cut-throats who form the Papal army occasionally interrupt these scenes of rural felicity, but when the tyrants appear the chief brigand always blows a horn, and a sufficient number of heroic patriots spring to all appearance out of the earth. It is a curious fact that, in spite of the most thrilling hairbreadth escapes, none of the virtuous are ever killed or seriously injured till the last chapter, when a general massacre takes place amongst the men, and the ladies go off to wait for a regenerated Italy.

We would fain hope that the stuff we have been describing was not really written by Garibaldi, but that some hoax has been practiced upon the translator and publisher. However, it is a fact that the book comes out with all the external appearance of authenticity, and that the circumstance of its bearing Garibaldi's name has been enough to secure for it favorable notices from writers who ought to know better. Garibaldi has suffered before now from the indiscretion of his intimates, and we fear he has on this occasion been flattered into an exhibition of weaknesses which will give cause of triumph to his enemies.

Garibaldi remained a favorite subject for other writers, especially those who liked action and drama. Besides Carducci and D'Annunzio, the Swedish poet Carl Snoilsky, and the German Ricarda Huch wrote about him. Tennyson gave him money (so did Lady Byron), and also wrote poetry in his honor. Swinburne once told a friend that Garibaldi was the greatest man since Adam (Georges Lafourcade, La Jeunesse de Swinburne, 1837–67, Paris, 1928, Vol. I, 187). The views of Henry Adams and George Sand have already been quoted. Mrs. Gaskell wrote a quiet but very sympathetic preface to Vecchi's account of his life on Caprera. Alexandre Dumas not only translated and "embellished" Garibaldi's memoirs, but followed the "Thousand" to Sicily, and there helped to manufacture red shirts on his yacht as he studied a real live hero as material for another novel. Victor Hugo was another great admirer, and was as delighted as he was astonished when, in reply to one of his odes on Garibaldi, there arrived in the post from Caprera a long poem written in French.

ELIZABETH BROWNING [3]

"My King, King Victor, I am thine!
So much Nice-dust as what I am

[3] From "Garibaldi" (1860), *The poetical works of Elizabeth Barrett Browning*, London, 1890, Vol. V, 35.

(To make our Italy) must cleave.
Forgive that." Forward with a sign
He went.
          You've seen the telegram?
Palermo's taken, we believe.

TENNYSON [4]

Or watch the waving pine which here
   The warrior of Caprera set,
   A name that earth will not forget
Till earth has roll'd her latest year.

SWINBURNE, AFTER THE DEATH OF ELIZABETH BARRETT BROWNING [5]

She saw not—happy, not seeing—
   Saw not as we with her eyes
Aspromonte; she felt
Never the heart in her melt
As in us when the news was dealt
Melted all hope out of being,
   Dropped all down from the skies.

CAROLINE PHILLIPSON [6]

Evviva Garibaldi! that honest soul and true;
Viva Italia una, though clouds obscure its blue;
And *à bas l'Intervention,* Napoleon's latest crime,
One which will cloud the prospects of France in future time.

Evviva Garibaldi! though in a prison-room
He sighs o'er Rome betrayèd, and mourns the captive's doom;

[4] Alfred Lord Tennyson, from "To Ulysses," (1864), *Demeter and Other Poems,* London, 1908, p. 78. (Garibaldi planted this tree for Tennyson in the Isle of Wight.)

[5] From "The Halt Before Rome: September 1867," in *The complete works of Algernon Charles Swinburne,* ed. Edmund Gosse and T. J. Wise, London, 1925, Vol. II, 114.

[6] From "The Battle of Mentana" (1867), by Caroline Gifford Phillipson, in *Mental Flights: A Volume of Verse, Political and Sentimental,* London, 1871, pp. 6–8.

Evviva Garibaldi! for in Mentana's fight
He bore him bravely for the cause of Liberty and Right. . . .

May the base Pontiff ruler, who sought for foreign aid,
Sink to his grave dishonour'd, forsaken and betray'd!
And ye, ye dames of Italy, have courage and be strong,
For light will gild the darken'd scene, and suns will shine ere long.

WHITTIER [7]

Rejoice, O Garibaldi! Though thy sword
Failed at Rome's gates, and blood seemed vainly poured
Where, in Christ's name, the crownèd infidel
Of France wrought murder with the arms of hell. . . .

God's providence is not blind, but full of eyes,
It searches all the refuges of lies;
And in His time and way, the accursed things
    Before whose evil feet thy battle-gage
    Has clashed defiance from hot youth to age
Shall perish. All men shall be priests and kings—
    One royal brotherhood, one church made free
    By love, which is the law of liberty!

MEREDITH [8]

The cry of Liberty from dungeon cell,
From exile, was his God's command to smite,
As for a swim in sea he joined the fight,
With radiant face, full sure that he did well.

Behold a warrior dealing mortal strokes,
Whose nature was a child's: amid his foes
A wary trickster: at the battle's close,
No gentler friend this leopard dashed with fox.

[7] John Greenleaf Whittier, from "Garibaldi," in *The Atlantic Monthly*, Boston, October, 1869, no. CXLIV, 431.

[8] George Meredith, from "The Centenary of Garibaldi" (1907), in *Poems*, London, 1910, Vol. III, 244.

PART THREE

GARIBALDI THROUGH THE EYES OF HISTORIANS

During his lifetime, Garibaldi was despised and feared by the official Italy of politicians and bien pensants, *even though an unwillingness to offend public opinion kept open criticism mostly in low key. It was almost as though people were embarrassed by the fact that they owed so much to such a simple (some would have said absurd and vulgar) person. Only when he could no longer trouble their dreams was he adopted by all and sundry and made into the legendary, archetypal Italian fighter for freedom and nationality. The number of those who claimed to have fought in his red-shirted brigades then began to multiply suspiciously. A catch-phrase entered the language (from a play by Edoardo Ferravilla, 1846–1916) about "never speaking ill of Garibaldi," as though criticism was now something too indecent to be contemplated.*

A slightly discordant note was sounded by an embittered conservative and catholic, Cesare Cantù, but his was still the voice of politics as much as of history. Some Catholics rather went out of their way to pay tribute to an opponent who had proved less devious and hypocritical than the conservative Italian politicians, and even Cantù was ready to call him the most effective in practice of all the patriotic leaders.

The most pungent and effective historical attack came not from that direction but from the American biographer of Cavour, W. R. Thayer. At the same time, it was foreign rather than Italian writers who became the high priests of the Garibaldi cult. Chief among these was the British historian, G. M. Trevelyan, who looked on Garibaldi's life as "the most poetical of all true stories," (An Autobiography and Other Essays, London, 1949, p. 13), *and on Garibaldi himself as one of the most effective and beneficent of all historical characters.*

But it was not only liberals and liberal-minded men such as Trevelyan who claimed this man. He was also annexed by the extreme Italian nationalists, for instance by D'Annunzio and Oriani, in whose eyes he became a lance with which to tilt against the drab parliamentarism of the new Italy. These nationalists did not much like Garibaldi's internationalism or his socialism, but they tried to overlook such humanitarian weaknesses by attributing them to his innocence and good nature. Even though D'Annunzio and Mussolini were both a little jealous of him and his reputation, it was still very important for them to appropriate as much as possible of the propaganda value of his name.

Ezio Garibaldi, a grandson, developed this line of thought to the point that Mussolini's conquest of power, after 1922, became merely a fulfilment of the patriotic, authoritarian tendencies in garibaldinismo; and, for him, the black shirts and the red shirts were in practice identical (Ezio Garibaldi, Fascismo Garibaldino, Rome, 1928, pp. 32–33). Later, the communists, not to be outdone, chose Garibaldi's face as their electoral emblem, in 1948, and so gained a number of adventitious votes—their opponents countered with a poster which showed Stalin peering out from behind a mask with Garibaldi's features.

Recent historians have reached more of a consensus. They have seen him not only as impossible to categorize in terms of fascism or communism, but as a man who was more liberal than his legend, a more balanced patriot than the self-styled "nationalists," and possessed of far more shrewdness and instinctive common sense than the conventional myth allowed.

15

An Obituary from the London *Times*, 1882[1]

Garibaldi is dead. The spell attached to his name
has partly been broken by the prolongation of his life beyond its
sphere of possible usefulness; but the worth of his character will
bear inspection, even when sober criticism had done its utmost to
strip it of all the glitter with which popular enthusiasm had in-
vested it.

In the first place, this hero of a hundred fights has been made
almost too much of as a warrior, but justice has hardly, perhaps,
been done to his abilities as a leader. Garibaldi was no strategist.
He knew little and cared less about organization, equipment, or
discipline; never looked to means of transport or commissariat, but
simply marched at the head of a few officers, hardly turning to see
how the troops would follow. He never had a competent head of
the staff. . . .

Garibaldi, however, was a tactician, and would have creditably
handled an army had a ready-made one, well-armed and trained
and led, been placed under his orders on the eve of battle. He had
the sure glance, the quick resolution, the prompt resource of that
enfant gâté de la victoire, his townsman Masséna [a marshal under
Napolean I]. As the Lombard volunteer Emilio Dandolo, quoted
by Dumas, graphically paints his chief—"On the approach of a foe,
Garibaldi would ride up to a culminating point in the landscape,
survey the ground for hours with the spy-glass in brooding silence,
and come down with a swoop on the enemy, acting upon some well-
contrived combination of movements by which advantage had been
taken of all circumstances in his favour." . . .

And it was in peace as in war. In leisure hours in his wanderings,
and more in his solitude at Caprera, Garibaldi read a good deal,
and accumulated an ill-digested mass of knowledge, of which the
utopian mysticisms of Mazzini and the paradoxical vagaries of

[1] *The Times,* June 5, 1882, pp. 5–6.

Victor Hugo constituted the chief ingredients. But, in politics as in arms, his mind lacked the basis of a rudimental education. He rushed to conclusions without troubling his head about arguments. His crude notions of Democracy, of Communism, of Cosmopolitanism, of Positivism, were jumbled together in his brain and jostled one another in hopeless confusion, involving him in unconscious contradiction notwithstanding all his efforts to maintain a character for consistency. In sober moments he seemed to acknowledge his intellectual deficiencies, his imperfect education, the facility with which he allowed his own fancy or the advice of dangerous friends to run away with his better judgment; but presently he would lay aside all diffidence, harangue, indite letters, preside at meetings, address multitudes, talk with the greatest boldness about what he least understood, and put his friends to the blush by his emphatic, trenchant, absolute tone, by his wild theories and sweeping assertions, as he did at Geneva at one of the Peace Society Congresses, when, before a bigoted Calvinistic audience, he settled the question whether St. Peter ever had or had not been in Rome—"a futile question," he said, "for I can tell you no such person as Peter has ever existed."

But with a heart like Garibaldi's a man may well afford to allow his brain to go a wool-gathering. As an earnest patriot—as all Italians were while a country was denied to them—Garibaldi never went wrong, or his error was repaired and atoned for before he had to rue its worst consequences. Let even his worst enemy write Garibaldi's biography and he will always appear the most single-minded and disinterested, the least self-conscious of all men. Not only did he for many years with unshaken consistency refuse all rewards and distinctions, but he shunned and dreaded popular clamour, and was worried and revolted, as well as confused and dismayed, at the abject worship paid to him by high and low wherever he appeared. He stood or sat stern and sullen, as women, men, and even priests in Calabria hailed him as "Our Messiah! Our Redeemer!"; as in Lombardy mothers held up their new-born infants to be christened by him, "no other hand being so sure to bring God's blessing with it;" or as in London, where, in 1864, he fairly ran away from the fine ladies who seemed at a loss to know how a true lion should be lionized.

Garibaldi had the ideal lion nature in him, all the dignity and gentleness, the sudden flash of anger, the forgiveness, the absence of all rancor, malice, or uncharitableness. Even the brute Leonardo Millan, who [in Brazil] had struck, racked, and imprisoned him without reason, when he fell into [Garibaldi's] power and trembled for his life, was suffered to go unscathed, the only vengeance of Garibaldi being limited to fixing his look into his face so as to give him to understand that he was recognized, but deemed utterly beneath a man's resentment.

He was the most loving, the least hating of men. Whatever follies or even crimes may have been committed in his name, one may freely defy the world to trace an act of meanness or a deed of cruelty, or even a deliberately unkind word, to the man himself. However madly he dabbled in republicanism, his devotion to Victor Emanuel was proof against all slight or ill-treatment on the part of the King's government. Whatever progress he made in the modern school of philosophers, his faith in God was unshaken. Unfortunately, his trust in men—and women—transcended all discretion. It is painful, but just, to record how his facile credulity entrapped him into a mock marriage with the Countess Raimondi, a young lady of rank, at Como, during the campaign of 1859 [*recte*, in January, 1860]; it is melancholy, but instructive, to recollect the spectacle he exhibited in Rome in 1874, when he made, for the first time, his appearance with a newly-wedded wife and babies in his suite, the results of his domestication with the nurse of his daughter's children [this new marriage was in 1880]. . . .

The veterans he brought with him from Montevideo [in 1848], a Genoese battalion whom his friend Augusto Vecchi helped to enlist, and the Lombard Legion, under Manara, were all men of tried valor, well trained to the use of the rifle, inured to hardships and privations, and they constituted the nucleus of the Garibaldian force throughout its campaigns. The remainder was a shapeless mass of raw recruits from all parts of Italy, joining or leaving the band almost at their pleasure—mere boys from the universities, youths of noble and rich family, lean artisans from the towns, stout peasants and laborers from the country, adventurers of indifferent character, deserters from the army, and the like, all marching in loose companies, like Falstaff's recruits, under improvised officers and non-commissioned officers; but all, or most of them, entirely disinterested about pay or promotion, putting up with long fasts and heavy marches, only asking to be brought face to face with the enemy, and when under the immediate influence of Garibaldi himself or of his trusty friends seldom guilty of soldierly excesses or of any breach of discipline. The effect the presence of the hero had among them was surprising. A word addressed to them in his clear, ringing, silver voice electrified even the dullest. An order coming from him was never questioned, never disregarded. No one waited for a second bidding or an explanation. "Your business is not to inquire how you are to storm that position. You must only go and do it." And it was done.

There was nothing more providential in the combination of favorable circumstances to which the triumph of the Italian cause was owing than the opportune production of this singular, this "mysterious conqueror," as he was called, and the almost mythical prestige he threw on deeds of arms so amazing in their success as to disarm criticism and to present them to the startled world in the light of superhuman achievements. When even the steady valor of the Piedmontese army, owing to bad generalship, was succumbing to the Austrian invader at Custoza and Novara, in 1848–9, it was something to say that mere citizens, under Garibaldi, were gloriously giving the lie to the old taunt that "Italians don't fight" by not only standing their ground behind stone walls at Venice and Rome, but also crossing bayonets with the best troops of the French Republic outside the gates of the latter-named city, and giving their lives with a lavishness worthy of the ancient warlike race whose dust lay beneath their feet. Garibaldi and Rome were all that survived as a hallowed memory out of the wreck of Italian hopes at that gloomy period; and Garibaldi and what remained of the heroes of Rome were what stood foremost in that more auspicious trial of 1859–60, in which the old errors were retrieved and the former disasters repaired. With the final emancipation of the country the three names of Victor Emanuel, Cavour, and Garibaldi will be for ever associated; but if the characters of the first and second of that triumvirate are sure to be deeply studied, thoroughly weighed, and rated at their just value as realities, the last-named will appeal to the imagination as something unauthenticated, like William Tell— a mere undemonstrable episode—a legend.

16
Two Conservative Views

CESARE CANTÙ [1]

Public opinion created an image of Garibaldi which cast him in the proportions not merely of a hero but of a god. No one, moreover, could think anything else but that a cause for which such sacrifices had been made must be generous and fine. To question this would have been an act of real courage. He was therefore compared to Lafayette; newspapers referred to him as "an archangel of war," "an angel of divine justice," "the Christ of our age"! People repaired the hut near Ravenna where in 1849 he had taken refuge with his dying wife, and it was said that the place would be revered in future like the stable of Bethlehem. Mordini, his pro-dictator in Sicily, decreed that the room at Palermo in which he had slept should be kept in perpetuity with all its existing furniture just as it was. Relics were stolen from him. Some people had no other ambition than to talk to him, or to be seen and recognized by him. . . .

At the other extreme some thought him childish, or even somewhat mad. When he made himself out to be a popular leader and above the law, this was blamed on parasites and courtiers who were said to be trying to increase his power in order to cover their own base interests and obtain for themselves an authority which they would never have won on their own. After these people had persuaded him that he was the apostle of humanity, he used to issue proclamations to the whole world, giving advice and even commands. He set himself up as the great life-giver, as the protector of Denmark against Germany, of the northern states in America against the South, of the Montenegrins against the Turks—and even of Jesus Christ against the Pope. . . .

Garibaldi was born among the people. Having no serious education, he had been forced to earn his living as a worker. He then

[1] Cesare Cantù, *Della indipendenza italiana, cronistoria,* Turin, 1878, Vol. III, part II, 580–83.

learned to set himself up as a kind of tribune of the people under the auspices of Mazzini. . . . Always he gave himself airs as though he were another Washington. . . . People lavished excessive praise on him because, in an egoistical world, he himself was not seeking a job, or a decoration, or money. Yet at the same time he could break out easily into vulgar outbursts which upset his friends and which were meat and drink to his detractors. As no one contradicted him, excessive praise only increased his self-esteem. . . .

Not for this man the ordinary procedures of liberal government. The only methods with which he was familiar were those of armed insurrection. He could destroy, but did not know how to build. Cattaneo once suggested to him at Palermo that he should issue certain decrees about copyright and mortgages, but he merely smiled and replied, "My sword will do all that has to be done."

Unlike Napoleon, who knew how to stop in front of difficulties, Garibaldi aimed after the impossible with the object of succeeding at all costs. As an honest and courageous man, he thought he could find heroism everywhere. He imagined that everyone was waiting to join him and that a million Italian volunteers would easily force Austria and even France to surrender. He posed as the apostle of every revolution, past and present, as the defender of all nationalities even those which did not exist. So confident was he in himself, that he assumed others must think as he did. And since he was sincere, his words carried weight; and sometimes indeed he was in the right however impractical or fantastic his beliefs may have seemed. He was not the kind of person who urges others to act so that he can then step in and take all the winnings, but on the contrary he tilted straight at his goal, ready to stand down and disappear as soon as it was reached.

ALFREDO ORIANI AND THE NATIONALIST MYTH [2]

In a century which began with Napoleon and ended with Moltke, it is almost puzzling to find this acclaim for Garibaldi who was little more than a soldier of fortune and never had more than a few battalions under his command. Garibaldi had learned nothing at school and left behind him nothing that the schools can study. He made his own career apparently out of nothing, and then again seemed to retreat into what was almost oblivion. He was a man who seemed to preach peace even in the middle of battle, who

[2] Alfredo Oriani, *Fino a Dogali* [1889], Bologna, 1912, pp. 22–26.

created a nation with a small group of soldiers, who founded a monarchy though proclaiming himself a republican, who gave liberty to peoples and kingdoms to kings, who conquered a fatherland for Italians and yet lost his own homeland of Nice, who openly challenged and defeated the Papacy, and then supported the French republic against the German empire.

Garibaldi died at Caprera as poor and as bare as the rock on which he had made his home. This is the Garibaldi that the officers of regular armies derided, whom ministers despised, the man who even the common people latterly seemed to abandon; and yet when he died he took on an incredible grandeur so as even to outclass Napoleon and Moltke themselves. The whole world admired him, from young America to the ancient civilizations of Asia. . . .

If Italy had not produced Mazzini and Garibaldi we would not have reappeared as a nation. These two are the real representatives of a new Italy reborn for a second time. They inaugurated a new era in world history. Every country has since then tried to claim them. Every liberal movement in the first half of this century took place in their names, every defeat shed a little of their blood, and in every victory we can recognize something of their genius.

It was our Latin race which made the French Revolution with Danton, and which then destroyed feudal Europe by means of Napoleon; subsequently it was to create liberal Europe through the medium of Garibaldi and Mazini. Meanwhile the same Italian genius which had inspired the ancient Roman empire taught everyone, through the skill of Cavour, how discipline and political compromise were indispensable conditions for ultimate political success. But Cavour had many rivals in this field among his contemporaries, even though no one else was quite as successful as he—there were Gladstone in England, Bismarck in Prussia, Frère Orban in Belgium, Gambetta in France, and all these showed a parliamentary and diplomatic skill which was as deep and creative as Cavour's. But the Italian revolution was, and will remain for ever, incarnate in Garibaldi and Mazzini. Here were Hercules and Prometheus, and now all the greater in proportion as the world of today is superior to that of ancient Greece.

17
The Liberal Enthusiasts

GARIBALDI AS A SOLDIER: BY CARLO TIVARONI [1]

Garibaldi learned how to fight in South America where distances were vast and soldiers were so few that large battles never took place. There he learned the technique of partisan warfare and to rely on frequent, rapid attacks. He lacked that special knowledge of war which others acquire from books or from the practice of large-scale fighting. As Carlo Corsi wote in his *Venticinque anni in Italia,* although Garibaldi always possessed a good strategical plan in his campaigns, on the level of tactics he acted more like a guerrilla leader than a regular general. He certainly did not lack a natural disposition to command, and he usually knew what to do, but he did lack the experience of commanding large numbers of regular troops. What he was accustomed to was small groups and small-scale wars.

It is said that the Austrian General D'Aspre told a Piedmontese official at Parma in 1848 that, "the one man who could have powerfully helped you in your war you completely ignored—Garibaldi." Probably this was just a newspaper story without factual basis, and in any case it could only have been a very summary judgment. One thing we should always remember is that Garibaldi at this period never had the chance of leading experienced and well disciplined troops, but had to make do with volunteers hastily improvised in a few weeks, and with officers and men who had no other training but what could be fitted in between one march and another. . . .

If we look at the events of 1859, on the other hand, we will see Garibaldi obediently taking part in a proper military plan of cam-

---

[1] Carlo Tivaroni, *Storia critica del risorgimento italiano,* Turin, 1897, Vol. IX, 506–9. Tivaroni, as well as being a distinguished historian, had fought with Garibaldi in 1866.

paign. In 1860, moreover, we can observe him carrying out miracles of both strategy and tactics. This shows that he had thought and learned a good deal between 1848 and 1859.

It is true that it was not his real nature to act as a subordinate general, for he did not like obeying blindly as a subordinate must do; at the same time he had other qualities which no other Italian general possessed in combination—and few foreigners. First of all he had a marvellously quick eye, something not learned from books. Just as with a doctor, if you do not have this by nature, you cannot learn it from studying or from practical experience. He had a quick appreciation of terrain, whereby he could speedily measure the precise extent of a battlefield, the strength of the enemy forces, the weak point of the opposing commander. On top of this he had extreme speed in taking decisions and acting on them. Occasionally, it is true, these decisions were rash, but almost always they were successful. Even in the midst of complete confusion he kept an imperturbable serenity, and this went along with an iron constitution, great liveliness, and energy. . . . Sometimes, as in the Trentino in 1866, he had to rely almost entirely on maps, and here his mathematical knowledge must have been a great help.

The faculty of never being rattled, of never letting himself be surprised, went with a coolness and an instinct for smelling out danger. General Manteuffel, in his history of the Franco-German war of 1870, particularly picks out Garibaldi's rapidity of tactical movements, his sensible dispositions during a battle, and his fiery energy in attack. All this, to be sure, in part depended on the temper of the soldiers under his command, so said Manteuffel; but it also showed a general who never for one moment forgot that the main objective is to dislodge the enemy from his positions, and as quickly as possible. . . .

Garibaldi used to be able to produce the maximum result with the minimum means. His own self-confidence was enough to make others believe that they could do exceptional deeds even with defective material. It was his doing if the middle and lower classes in Italy, who for centuries had not been accustomed to fighting, now learned to take arms for their fatherland and recognized the importance of obedience, discipline, courage, and sticking together. Garibaldi's volunteers referred to him, quite simply, as "the general," and they were right; for he was the only great general that Italy produced in the whole course of the *risorgimento*.

TREVELYAN AND THE LIBERAL APOTHEOSIS

Garibaldi had, perhaps, the most romantic life that history records, for it had all the trappings as well as the essence of romance. Though he lived in the nineteenth century, it was yet his fortune never to take full part in the common prose life of civilized men, and so he never understood it, though he moved it profoundly, like a great wind blowing off an unknown shore. He never had education, either intellectual, diplomatic, or political; even his military training was that of the guerilla chief; nor, till he was past learning, did he experience the ordinary life of the settled citizen. Though all must acknowledge that, by the secret ordering of the mysteries of birth, he had been created with more in him of the divine than any training can give, yet we cannot fail to perceive, in studying the slight records of the first forty years of his life, how much the natural tendencies of his genius, in their strength and in their weakness, were enhanced by circumstance.

And so, when in 1848 he returned to fight for Italy, in the full strength of matured manhood—at the time of life when Cromwell first drew sword—he had been sheltered, ever since he went to sea at fifteen, from every influence which might have turned him into an ordinary man or an ordinary soldier.

He had two schools—the seas of romance, and the plateaus of South America. He had lived on ship-board and in the saddle. The man who loved Italy as even she has seldom been loved, scarcely knew her. The soldier of modern enlightenment was himself but dimly enlightened. Rather, his mind was like a vast sea cave, filled with the murmur of dark waters at flow and the stirring of nature's greatest forces, lit here and there by streaks of glorious sunshine bursting in through crevices hewn at random in its rugged sides.[2]

All schools of Italian historians are, I think, agreed that the Sicilian and Neopolitan populations had proved incopable of effecting a revolution in the face of an army of 90,000 men, without external help; that Cavour was unable, owing to the attitude of Europe, and in particular of France and Austria, to give that help with the regular forces of the North Italian kingdom; that nothing, therefore, could have liberated Sicily and Naples except an irre-

[2] George Macaulay Trevelyan, *Garibaldi's Defence of the Roman Republic*, London, 1907, pp. 23-24. Reprinted with the permission of Longmans, Green & Co. Limited.

sponsible "raid" by volunteers of the revolutionary party, and that no such "raid" could have succeeded except one led by Garibaldi; finally, that it was only the Garibaldian revolution in Sicily and Naples that put Cavour into the position from which he ventured, in the face of Europe, to attack the Pope's possessions in Umbria and the Marches, and so to unite the whole length of the peninsula in one continuous state. . . .

There is, for the historian, an unique interest in the detailed study of the Garibaldian epic. We can make no such minute inquiry into the lives of Wallace and Tell, and of others who resembled him both in the nature of their work as liberators, patriots and partisan warriors, and in the romantic and old-world circumstances of their achievements. The records of Wallace and the dimmer legends of Tell are so meager that they leave on us the impression of the heroic figures of Flaxman's outlines, with certain noble stories attached to their names. Even the fuller records of Joan of Arc, to whom Treitschke compared Garibaldi, date from a time so far back in the infancy of historical method, that in our day the learned can still dispute as to the nature of the influences which she underwent herself, and exerted over others. But the records of the Italian national hero and his deeds are detailed to the point of realism. We possess such a mass of evidence, official and unofficial, printed, written and oral, of his friends and his enemies, his followers and his opponents in the field, that we certainly do not lack the material to fill in a living picture of the man and his achievements.

How then, examined in so clear a light, do the legendary exploits of Garibaldi appear? Does the surrounding atmosphere of poetry and high idealism, when considered curiously, evaporate like a mirage? Or does it not rather take shape as a definite historical fact, an important part of the causes of things and a principal part of their value? To my mind the events of 1860 should serve as an encouragement to all high endeavor amongst us of a later age, who, with our eyes fixed on realism and the doctrine of evolution, are in some danger of losing faith in ideals, and of forgetting the power that a few fearless and utterly disinterested men may have in a world where the proportion of cowards and egoists is not small.[3]

Garibaldi's claim on the memory of men rests on more than his actual achievements. It rests on that which was one part of his pro-

[3] George Macaulay Trevelyan, *Garibaldi and the Thousand*, London, 1909, pp. 5–7. Reprinted with the permission of Longmans, Green & Co. Limited.

fessional equipment as a soldier of revolution, but which surpasses and transcends it—his appeal to the imagination. He was a poet, in all save literary power. He was guided in political, and somewhat even in military situations, by a poet's instincts and motives. He is perhaps the only case, except Byron for a few weeks in Greece, of the poet as man of action. For most poets, if they ever take part in action, cease to be poetical. While he was alive this quality was both his strength and his weakness—Samson's locks and Achilles' heel. But now that he is dead, the poetry in his character and career is all gain in his race for immortal laurels. The history of events is ephemeral and for the scholar; the poetry of events is eternal and for the multitude. It is the acted poem that lives in the hearts of millions to whom the written words of history and the written words of poetry are alike an unopened book. So Garibaldi becomes the symbol of *Italia* to her children in all ages to come and on either side of the Atlantic.[4]

[4] George Macaulay Trevelyan, *Garibaldi and the Making of Italy*, London, 1911, pp. 296–97. Reprinted with the permission of Longmans, Green & Co. Limited.

18

Two Views on the Controversy Between Cavour and Garibaldi in 1860–61

Garibaldi's Red Shirts risked life and fortune on their splendid enterprise: was it becoming that, even before they had finished their task, they should begin to clamor for rewards? Was it edifying to see them through Garibaldi's agency attempt to seize the State by the throat and bid it yield or perish? Why is it that the very men who, in an ecstasy of devotion, sacrifice everything in order to save or to create a nation, will not sacrifice their selfish claims when they have weathered the crisis? Better, a thousand times better, like Leonidas and his Three Hundred, to sleep in glory on the field of a lost battle, enshrined forever in the gratitude of mankind, than to go forth under the spell of patriotism at the call of duty, and, having performed deeds of undying lustre, to come back and pose as heroes, demanding pensions and honors and offices, and by vanity and greed to make patriotism odious!

But the indictment against Garibaldi goes deeper than his hatred of Cavour; it concerns Italy herself. National unification was achievable only through the cooperation of the two elements—the Monarchy and the Revolution. By promoting the National Society, and by enlisting Garibaldi on the side of the Monarchy, Cavour secured this indispensable cooperation. Garibaldi undertook to lead the Revolution in the name of the Monarchy, but though loyal at heart to the King, he rebelled against the policy of the King's government. Dictatorial by nature, he neither understood nor respected the prosaic working of a constitutional régime. Relying on his emotions, with hardly the reasoning power of a child, he despised or resolved to ignore facts which, like his bug-bear, Diplomacy, he found inconvenient.

Tested by the touchstone of patriotism, his mad outbreak in Parliament [April 18, 1861] must be unqualifiedly condemned: for he made the interest of his few thousand volunteers paramount to the welfare of Italy: to sacrifice all to a clique is not patriotism. If they had been unjustly treated, they might have waited to have their wrongs redressed. But Garibaldi, in order to get commissions for his officers and pay and a billet for his soldiers, was ready—although he did not realize it—to wreck his country. . . .

His obsession of hatred for Cavour, his innate megalomania, his inability to reason, from which came his lack of historical perspective, his accessibility to flatterers, his unwavering devotion to whatever plan he adopted, and his certitude that whatever he planned was the final evangel of patriotism, predestined him to threaten the very existence of Italy in April, 1861. If it be argued that he served Italy by goading the reluctant forward and by enabling Cavour to hasten unification by scaring Diplomacy with the spectre of the Revolution, the reply is yes: but Garibaldi might have done this service without adopting the policy of hatred which so greatly impaired his achievement. Much more was involved than the explosion of his personal wrath. The Party of Action made him their tool. They hoped, under cover of his immense prestige, to shape the foreign policy of the new Kingdom; as they might have done, had their move for the enrolment of a half-million volunteers, to be led by him, been successful.

In resisting him and them, at the risk of his own popularity and, as it proved, of his life, Cavour performed the best service that a patriot could perform at that crisis. As in the previous October, so now he carried the contest into Parliament, an arena which Garibaldi could not decline, although he was placed at as great a disadvantage there as his statesmen adversaries would have been in the saddle. Cavour showed by this that under a constitutional régime no man, not even the monarch, is above the law: that was the stern lesson which the Italians, and Garibaldi above all, most needed to learn.[1]

It was Garibaldi, Crispi and Bertani who took on the principal risk and responsibility of failure over this revolution in the south. These radical enthusiasts would have been mercilessly killed had they failed, and as mercilessly condemned by Italians and by history. As events turned out, it was their misfortune to be blamed even for their success. Cavour was always quite ready to disown them, and indeed he even expected to do so; and they knew as much and were content. Looking ahead to Aspromonte and Mentana one

[1] William Roscoe Thayer, *The Life and Times of Cavour*, Boston, 1911, Vol. II, 479-81.

can see what might easily have happened in 1860. Cavour's successors twice allowed or incited Garibaldi to risk his life and the future of Italy, but subsequently had to order their troops to fire upon and wound him, to arrest him and his men, and then to cover him with the obloquy of failure. This was what Garibaldi knowingly risked again and again.

If he had been ambitious for himself, his conduct would not have been so admirable; but he was in everything unostentatious, not least in his graceful surrender of office in November; and when in April 1861 Musolino proposed in parliament to make him a gift from the nation, this proposal had to be withdrawn at Garibaldi's own wish. If he had not dutifully obeyed the king, this too would have made him lack something of greatness. But he was as loyal in obedience as he was resolute in command. There were many of the trappings of vulgar dictatorship about him; and yet one must not leave out of account how he impressed men of intellect as well as of action with his claims to be considered a liberal and essentially a good man. . . .

Garibaldi had an instinctive understanding of some southern problems, an understanding which often escaped observers in the north. Unlike the Piedmontese conservatives, for instance, he had the good sense to see that Mazzini presented no danger to law and order in Naples, except perhaps in so far as the "moderates" might stir up popular riots against him. Garibaldi understood both Mazzini and the south better than Cavour ever did, for the same reason that he had much more knowledge of and sympathy with the common people. Instead of assuming that southerners were idle and corrupt, and instead of trying to impose a cut-and-dried system upon them, he had worked by appealing to their good nature; and this had evoked a far more positive response than greeted his more technically efficient successors. What he gave them was enthusiasm, faith in a cause, and a fine example of self-sacrifice and courage. These were the very qualities which Mazzini all along had said were necessary for making Italians conscious of their strength, for making them politically conscious and politically responsible. Mazzini's chief objection to the Cavourian system was that it did not start by teaching the nation an awareness of its nationhood, and did not go on to persuade the common people that they ought to co-operate in building their own nation. The party of Cavour was in general ignorant and frightened of the common people, and preferred to impose its will with the aid of diplomacy, rather than to rouse this sleeping giant and give it ideas above its station. . . .

The radicals in southern Italy had proved the common people to be a superb initiating force. In the eyes of the populace, Garibaldi was a hero who brought out the best in them: he stood for all that seemed good in the *risorgimento*, all that was heroic, romantic, honest, and "popular" in the sense of "of the people"; while Cavour, for all his skill and success, stood for many of its worst aspects, for what was matter-of-fact, for duplicity, lack of generosity, for shady bargains with Louis Napoleon, and all that was double-faced and deceitful. Early in 1861 some of the deputies had to conclude that Garibaldi would not have been so bad after all as a royal viceroy in the south; and though historians have usually ridiculed Garibaldi's offer to take this post, he could hardly have done much worse than Farini and most of his many successors. At least there would probably have been a more friendly and enthusiastic spirit in Naples and Sicily. People would not so easily have been able to say afterwards that the great majority of Italian citizens were quite detached from, and uninterested in, the movement for national independence.[2]

[2] D. Mack Smith, *Cavour and Garibaldi, 1860,* Cambridge, 1954, pp. 441–43. Reprinted with the permission of Cambridge University Press.

19

Mussolini Acknowledges His Predecessor, May, 1932[1]

Your Majesty! Our gracious Queen!

On the Janiculan hill, this essentially Garibaldian territory [where Garibaldi fought the French onslaught upon Rome, in 1849], the fascist government has now erected a monument to the memory of Anita. It depicts her as a mother protecting her child, but at the same time as a guerrilla fighter galloping after the fleeing enemy. The artist has here given us the innermost soul as well as the outward features of Anita, for throughout her short, adventurous life she showed how to reconcile and combine the high duties of motherhood with those of the intrepid fighter who was Garibaldi's companion at arms.

We are now celebrating the fiftieth anniversary of the hero's death with national solemnity. We are here to inaugurate this monument in Your August Presence, along with the descendants of Garibaldi and his brave veterans. It is an occasion on which the whole Italian people is with us here in spirit.

Not only is Garibaldi an historical figure, but he lives on in the soul of the multitude. This was said before his death and it has been said since, in history books, in art, in poetry and legend. As adolescents we learned to look on this man in the light of his legend, and as grown men the power of reason has not diminished the enthusiasm that once warmed our hearts. As people of a new century, and at a long remove from his successes, we claim the right and the duty to remember and honor him.

We fascists are able to claim this right and this duty, just because we bravely stood alongside a few Garibaldians for the cause of intervention in the first world war. Indeed it was we who imposed that war on Italians and carried it through to final victory. It was

[1] *Opera omnia di Benito Mussolini*, ed. Edoardo and Duilio Susmel, Florence, 1958, Vol. XXV, 108–11. Reprinted with the permission of Casa Editrice La Fenice.

we who then shed our blood to protect the fruits of that victory and make it part of our inalienable national heritage.

We live in exceptional and very difficult times. Yet we Italians who acted in this way are not just a few. There are millions of us from one end of the country to the other, disciplined *en masse* as fighters for the first time since the days of the Roman Empire. Between 1914 and 1918, we twentieth-century Italians, under Your leadership Sire, took up the march which Garibaldi in 1866 interrupted at Bezzecca when he replied to the government's order to retreat with his short, dramatic telegram, "I obey." We have now continued that march as far as the Brenner frontier on the Alps, as far as Trieste, Fiume, the island of Zara, and the crest of the Monte Nevoso. We have even carried the fight to the far shores of the Adriatic.

The blackshirts who fought and died in those years of humiliation [immediately before the fascist revolution in 1922] are legitimate descendants of the redshirts and their great *condottiero*. All his life long Garibaldi's heart was aflame with a single passion, as he fought for the unity and independence of the fatherland. Never did he give way, never was he forced to surrender his high ideal—not by men, nor by the sects, not by parties or ideologies, nor by the declamation encountered in parliamentary assemblies. These assemblies Garibaldi despised, advocate as he was of an "unlimited" dictatorship in difficult times. . . .

In Garibaldi's life, as in every other, action is inevitably accompanied by minor and unworthy acts of criticism, of ingratitude, even abandonment. This great man would have lacked something of greatness had he not also remained an ordinary mortal among ordinary mortals. But history has already weighed up the pros and cons and given its definitive sentence. Garibaldi is thereby all the greater; he is more alive, more lofty, and more powerful than ever in the conscience of the nation and of humanity. This present generation, which feels the weight of those bloody experiences suffered in the greatest war in all history, can now turn to Garibaldi with a much clearer eye and one no longer clouded by the political passions of his day.

Italy has acquired a frontier along the Alps and we shall never surrender it. We have carried our flag and our civilization into the heart of Africa, and are now preparing to live a yet more ample life than before. We Italians love and extol Garibaldi as the mariner of the oceans, as the general who won so many victories and yet who was compelled to stop short of so much he might have achieved, as the man who offered to his redshirts not honors and decorations, but "a tent as your roof, the bare earth as your bed, and God for the only witness of your deeds." This was a man who knew the solitude of prison, yet also experienced a veritable apotheosis when he travelled to London in 1864.

Garibaldi used to describe himself as a farmer. In the interval between battles, and in the twilight of his life, he liked to live among farmers, as he liked hard toil on the land. Before his death he even worked on a scheme for draining the Pontine marshes round Rome. Here was someone who disdained honors and riches, who remained poor as an anchorite, and yet was more generous than Caesar himself. In him were subsumed and sublimated the best qualities of the Italian people, together with those which are peculiar to his home province of Liguria, whose inhabitants are so solid and courageous, practical and yet idealistic.

Fifty years have passed since the day when that courageous heart stopped beating, since the moment when his eyes closed after a sweet and ultimate vision of his children. That solitary island of Caprera has since then become one of the sacred places of our fatherland, and so it will always remain.

Your Majesty, and our gracious Queen, if only this bronze figure which rides here before us could open its eyes once again in life, I think it would recognize as the true heirs of Garibaldi's redshirts those soldiers who won at Vittorio Veneto [in 1918] and our blackshirts who for the last few years have made his idea of voluntary service more popular and more productive than ever. With what pleasure he would look upon our present-day Rome, luminous, vast, no longer torn by factions, this Rome which he so deeply loved and which from his earliest youth he always identified with Italy!

Your Majesty, so long as this statue of our Hero dominates this hill, strong and certain will remain the destiny of our fatherland! (*The Duce had hardly finished speaking when the crowd burst into applause, and their emotion had a moment of stupendous grandeur when the Duce turned and suddenly saw at his side Ezio Garibaldi, and embraced him and kissed him twice. A wave rippled through the red sea of Garibaldians beneath him, and the great cry went up from those massed peoples of* "Duce! Duce!")

20

A Modern Reassessment, Virgilio Titone[1]

In Italy more than elsewhere there is a temptation to argue like this: Garibaldi was a hero; therefore he *must* have been somewhat crude, obtuse and ignorant. And sometimes the argument is taken to such a pitch that he is made out to be almost a simpleton or weak in the head. Such an interpretation, however, leaves unsolved the problem—and it is a real problem—how such a man could have become so idolized by masses of people all over the world. To cite one among a thousand examples, why was it that Alessandro Manzoni [the most distinguished writer in 19th-century Italy], who was as far removed as anyone could be from rhetoric and mere fashionable enthusiasms, why did he almost prostrate himself at Garibaldi's feet as he did on the latter's visit to Milan [in 1862]? Why did Lincoln offer him a command in the civil war against the South? Why did Lassalle [the German socialist], who was no fool, travel to consult Garibaldi at Caprera; and why did Kossuth [the patriotic leader of Hungary] look to Garibaldi for the liberation of his own people? England, too, Victorian England at the height of its glory, with its lords, dukes, ministers and poets, they all accorded him almost superhuman honors. Were all these people mad, or were Garibaldi's theatrical talents such as to confuse the most acute brains of his time? . . .

Garibaldi was much sharper and more perceptive, as he was also much closer to the concrete realities of contemporary Italy, than most of the leading figures of our *risorgimento*. It is not quite accurate to say that he believed in the people. What he believed in was practical action; and here he was proved right. Compare this with the way that the most consummate politicians, the most astute and prudent diplomats, so often calculated wrongly; whereas he, on the other hand, calculated correctly, and the expedition of

[1] Virgilio Titone, *Quaderni reazionari no. 2*, Palermo, February, 1963, pp. 52–56, 62–65. Reprinted with the permission of Virgilio Titone.

the Thousand was just one example of what that meant in practice. He was not a man of dogma as Mazzini was. His acceptance of hard facts—for example his acceptance of the monarchy and the army of Piedmont—shows a more open and more flexible intelligence than Mazzini possessed. He may not have had a political system in the way that Mazzini, Gioberti, and others had a system; but can one say that Mazzini, with his cloudy ideas about God and people, or Gioberti who shared the belief of Mazzini and many other European romantics in a special mission of certain peoples, can one say that either of these two showed more perception than a person who had no patience with such metaphysical nonsense? No doubt their ideas, though philosophically and politically empty, did possess a certain practical importance as propaganda; nonetheless on this plane one must admit that the myth which Garibaldi created about himself was not a whit less effective.

Some people deny him any qualities as a strategist and think of him merely as a pirate or gang-leader. But is it not possible that a pirate could incidentally possess the same qualities of command as a Nelson? And what else were Drake, or Khair ad-din Barbarossa [in the 16th century], but pirates? Is it really true that commanding a small band or winning a skirmish are invariably easier than defeating the enemy in open battle with a large army? Garibaldi in fact did not command just small bands, nor did he win just skirmishes, but even if this were true his hundred victories, small and large, could not be attributed only to good luck. His march on Palermo in 1860 was worthy of the very greatest general.

His later conduct in Sicily, too, for instance the skill with which he made himself the idol of the common people, with his instinctive knowledge of their wishes and their changeableness, and the fact of his attending religious ceremonies to the great scandal of his volunteers, all this shows some political shrewdness. One must note his outstanding skill in the way he exercised a fascination on others, and the ability by which, if necessary, he could impose his will on nobles and common people alike. He proved that he was as much at home in the palaces of the conventional English aristocracy as he was among the rough sailors and semi-pirates of Montevideo, and yet he was admired equally in both spheres. Does all this not show that, along with his other abilities, he possessed a clear appreciation of different situations, a real feeling for the circumstances in any particular moment where he might find himself having to take action?

Ordinary mortals bear a mask that can never be entirely put aside, and this it is which gives the singleness and unilateral quality that goes to make an individual character. But real genius—and there is a genius in action as there is another in thought and art—can take on many guises. Herein lies Garibaldi's fascination. Everyone can find in him something of themselves. Bandi tells us that many of his volunteers could stoop to almost anything on occasion, but as soon as he appeared they fell silent, and one look from him was enough to restore discipline even among the most refractory. Can one say that it was just his South American poncho which gave him the ability to command such men and with such good effect? . . .

One must remember that, to all effects and purposes, there were only 20,000 or 30,000 Italians altogether who counted for much at the time, and therefore with a thousand or merely a few hundred people it was possible to change the fate of the whole peninsula. The facts show this to have been so, and this helps to explain and justify the continuous agitation which Garibaldi and his friends kept alive, an agitation which otherwise might seem excessively foolhardy and adventurous. Many people never understood this. Cavour, for example, never understood it, nor did Mazzini, nor did Pisacane who made himself out to be such a profound strategist. These last two used to speak of a war of the people, but they understood neither war nor the people. Garibaldi, on the other hand, understood both, and in addition was a genuine hero in a sense they were not.

One can see this in his Sicilian campaign. Crispi, Rosolino Pilo, and other Sicilians had promised him the support of innumerable bands of insurgents who would join his forces, but when he landed he found no sign of them. Several days after the landing, when he reached Salemi, he encountered a group of peasants who seemed almost like wild savages, and their first request was to know which side would give them money and how much. But Garibaldi did not pay any attention. "You will see," he told Bandi, "that once we are seen to be winning, those who are now merely watching us will join our ranks." And in fact it happened just as he said. He knew that one must begin by winning, and that for this initial victory he could count on no one. Here was a fundamental fact. In this sense it was absolutely vital to know the people and know how much they could be counted on. Mazzini and some others used to imagine that they could guide insurrection from a distance, while Pisacane just counted on people who he thought *ought* to have joined him. Garibaldi, on the other hand, trusted just in himself and his few followers, and so was victorious. . . .

In this way he reflected his age better than anyone else. . . . It was through him alone that the revolution finally succeeded in practice. In 1820 in Naples and Sicily, in 1821 in Piedmont, later at Modena with Ciro Menotti, and then in 1848 all over Italy, there had been a belief that revolutionaries could work with the support of kings and dynasties; or at least it was thought that some of the ruling families would support the revolution once it had begun. Or else, if they did not trust in kings or in the Pope, these early revolutionaries had placed their confidence in a hypothetical or imaginary abstraction which they dubbed "the people," and simply assumed that these people would rebel. But they did not stop to ask who these people were or what they wanted. Mazzini shared this particular confidence. His expedition into Savoy [in 1833], and those other sad occasions when the brothers Bandiera died [in 1844] and when Pisacane was killed at Sapri [in 1857], all these proved that Mazzini's faith was unjustified.

Garibaldi was the only one who understood the real situation and acted consistently. He alone was capable of giving to those thousands (thousands rather than millions) who formed the "real Italy" a positive creed and an unhoped-for power. He was brave enough to fight and to rely only on his own forces, even though he sometimes had to combat not only the enemy but also the deceitfulness of the Piedmontese government which claimed to be his friend. This happened in Sicily, and again afterwards at Naples. One must not make too much of the so-called "letters of *marque*" or permissions to act which were granted to him by the government. These are sometimes said to have been the way in which an essentially powerless Garibaldi carried out what in fact were merely the designs of others. But the truth is different. Always round Garibaldi there was a crowd of Italians and foreigners demanding that he should start some revolutionary movement. But the real brains were his, and it was he who decided whether and when to act. In this connection, however, one must not forget the highly prosaic fact that action needed money, and Garibaldi did not have any; hence he needed some kind of permission to act from people in authority.

When the Thousand embarked at Quarto [in May 1860], Garibaldi's first observation was that a thousand men were too many.

Nor, as I have explained already, did he reckon on receiving local military support in Sicily. On their own, these thousand men landed at Marsala to find it a deserted city, and then marched to Calatafimi where they won their first victory. It was a decisive battle. Even though other victories lay ahead, it was Calatafimi which decided the fate of the whole expedition. And how did he win?— by courage, a quick eye and quick decisions, always anticipating the enemy and taking the offensive. Other people, on the contrary, would have preferred plans and calculation; others preferred to work by the book and so would have acted with prudence or timidity. But Garibaldi was the one who issued victorious. And among the reasons for his victory there is certainly the fact that he had not studied in any formal military academy, nor had his subordinate generals, Sirtori, Cosenz and the others who later showed themselves to be the best officers in the whole Italian army.

Garibaldi thus made himself into what could be called a great Power in his own right. At any moment he had at his disposal some thousand or so men, the equivalent of what today might be a hundred times as many, and everyone was aware that these few knew how to fight and die. He also possessed a weapon which no other Power at the time possessed so effectively. This weapon, the atomic bomb of those times, was public opinion, then at its most powerful. Sometimes public opinion proved quite irresistible, for it could start a movement which could rapidly run from one end of the world to another. Subsequently things changed and it would no longer be so easy for a few people to have such power. The future was, in time, to bring universal suffrage, party organization and propaganda. Large-scale industry would then create a new ruling class, and increase the power of money. Mass readership would create the modern press and increase the power of the written word. Railways, too, and the conservative deadweight of modern bureaucracy, these would also help to make it less easy for a few people to have such authority over people's minds. But in those days in Sicily, someone who could read was a one-eyed man in a world of the blind, just because he could read the newspaper to his illiterate friends when it arrived from the big city. The illiterate, the blind, just because they could not see, did not talk. The few people who could talk were everything.

This is why, notwithstanding some appearances, the *squadrismo* of D'Annunzio's march on Fiume [in 1919] and Mussolini's on Rome [in 1922] were to be something quite different, for the whole context had changed by then. They were not the *risorgimento* but the anti-*risorgimento*. They were the negation of that confidence in humanity which made the poetry and the soul of the romantic movement. However you try to justify fascism, it was always to stand for exaltation of brute force, for *sacro egoismo;* it was prose and not poetry. The way in which Italy had become a united state created certain inherent weaknesses in society—for example it tended to leave the Left unintegrated and in opposition. This in turn brought increasing discredit on parliamentary institutions and governments, while there was also a growing tendency to prefer the politics of brute force and rioting in the streets. But, of all this, Garibaldi and *garibaldinismo* were not even the putative fathers. The *risorgimento* was what it was just because contemporary attitudes, and the situation of Italy at the time, allowed so much and no more. The restless agitation of the Garibaldians, which kept the King's ministers in such a state of alarm, had a positive function in that earlier period, because it pushed the king along the road which led to Rome and hastened the process by which Italy was finally made.

Afterword

Garibaldi lived long enough to suffer some disillusionment with his handiwork. "It was a very different Italy which I spent my life dreaming of," so he wrote in 1880, "not the impoverished and humiliated country which we now see ruled by the dregs of the nation" (*Edizione Nazionale degli Scritti*, Vol. VI, 306). This pessimism was sharpened by considerable physical suffering and a sense of political impotence. The radical Left continued to acknowledge his honorary leadership (*Discorsi parlamentari di Felice Cavallotti*, Rome, 1914, Vol. II, 177), but these radicals were individualists without power and remained impenitently outside the world of machine politics. The machine was bound to take over from the individualists as the country settled down. The essential role of Garibaldi and the radicals after 1870 was, therefore, just to provoke, to challenge, to force the pace, and also to insert some ordinary humanity into the workings of politics; but they lacked the political sense and the sheer patience needed to realize their ideal dream of a more socially stable Italy. By their nature, they were bound to oppose the system, and, in their opposition, they did the most valuable job they could have done. But these latter years were the mere aftermath of victory; they were a prosaic period of reconstruction that inevitably followed and consolidated the poetic achievements of the *risorgimento* itself. The stirring days of battle came to an end with the occupation of Rome, in 1870. Garibaldi's active career virtually ended with this completion of national unity that he knew to have been his main mission in life.

After examining as much as possible of the evidence, the question remains of how important Garibaldi was in the making of Italy. Some people thought him merely an attractive, picturesque figurehead, possessed of little intrinsic significance. Richard Wagner once likened him to a fly caught in the great European spider's web (The memoirs of Malwida von Meysenbug, *Rebel in a Crinoline*, ed. M. Adams, London, 1937, p. 197). Other responsible observers, even in his own lifetime, compared him to George Washington, Joan of Arc, Robin Hood, William Tell, even to Luther and Mohammed (*The Westminster Review*, London, October, 1859, Vol. XVI, 479). Today, in a more distant retrospect, it may be easier to judge whether these contemporaries were too easily dazzled. Whether he stood for the right or the wrong, whether he was a proto-fascist or a liberal-minded democrat, to what degree he was sensible or foolish, far-sighted or narrowly selfish: these questions, too, must be brought to the test of documentary proof.

Garibaldi lacked a capacity for self-criticism. He was too innocent. No doubt he took himself too seriously; and no doubt there was too little thinking and too much declamation in his pronouncements. But he was incorruptible, even by power. As ruler of Sicily in 1860, he compares surprisingly well with the conservatives who succeeded him and who tried to justify themselves by depreciating his achievements. Whatever other qualifications may be made, it is hard to deny him the major share in conquering half of Italy, and in the collapse of the Pope's temporal power. Just as it is hard to deny that this single man attracted to Italian nationalism many politically powerful foreigners and many of the common people of Italy, so it is hard to deny that it was Garibaldi who made the conservatives become revolutionary patriots, who forced upon them the reality of a new political situation created by himself, and then compelled them to take over his program as their only hope of preventing his victory. In the process, he gave Italians self-confidence and a pride in achievement which they could hardly have obtained in any other way.

Bibliographical Note

Garibaldi's memoirs have appeared in several English versions. One was published by Theodore Dwight in New York, in 1859, the first instalment of his autobiography to be published anywhere. The following year, a fuller and somewhat different version was edited in French by Alexandre Dumas and at once translated into English, German, and Spanish. Subsequently, an "authorized" version as translated by A. Werner, *Autobiography of Giuseppe Garibaldi* (2 vols., London, 1889). This is, on balance, the best, especially as a third, supplementary volume was issued with the very interesting recollections of Garibaldi's English friend, Jessie White Mario. More recently, there has been a new edition of Dumas's version by R. S. Garnett, *The Memoirs of Garibaldi* (London, 1931). Garibaldi's first novel was also published in English as *The Rule of the Monk: or, Rome in the Nineteenth Century* (2 vols., London, 1870). Some other Garibaldi documents are translated in *The Making of Italy, 1796–1870* (ed. D. Mack Smith, New York, 1968).

A number of other relevant works in English have been mentioned earlier in this volume. In addition, one early biography by someone who knew him well is Colonel Chambers' *Garibaldi and Italian Unity* (London, 1864). Very good for a personal view of Garibaldi at home is C. A. Vecchi, *Garibaldi at Caprera* (Cambridge, 1862), and Elpis Melena, *Garibaldi: Recollections of his Public and Private Life* (London, 1887). Of recent biographies, the shortest is D. Mack Smith, *Garibaldi, a Great Life in Brief* (New York, 1956). There is also E. J. Parris, *The Lion of Caprera* (London, 1962), particularly useful on his early life. Less serious, but equally readable, is Christopher Hibbert, *Garibaldi and his Enemies* (London, 1965).

Much more important, however, are the three volumes of G. M. Trevelyan, *Garibaldi's Defence of the Roman Republic* (London,

1907), *Garibaldi and the Thousand* (London, 1909), *Garibaldi and the Making of Italy* (London, 1911), which have each run through some ten editions since their first publication. Trevelyan himself, in later life, thought that the first of these "bears the mark of something nearer to inspiration than I ever reached again." In the space of sixty years, some of his facts have, of course, been proved wrong, and he himself, in retrospect, somewhat modified his earlier enthusiasm; but this trilogy still remains the finest individual contribution to the subject in any language.

A new edition of Garibaldi's own miscellaneous writings has for some time been promised, but seems still to be in a preparatory stage. Previous editions omit a good deal and are not entirely accurate: this is true of E. E. Ximenes, *Epistolario di Giuseppe Garibaldi* (2 vols., Milan, 1885), and D. Ciàmpoli, *Giuseppe Garibaldi, Scritti Politici e Militari* (2 vols., Rome, 1907). The best available collection of Garibaldi's writings is that published by Cappelli of Bologna to celebrate the "Garibaldi year" decreed by Mussolini in 1932—*Edizione Nazionale Degli Scritti di Giuseppe Garibaldi* (ed. S. Di Marzo, A. Luzio, A. Monti, and others). This contains two different versions of the Memoirs, together with his autobiographical novel *I Mille* (1933), and three volumes of *Scritti e Discorsi Politici e Militari* (*1934–1937*). Another useful collection is M. Menghini, *La Spedizione Garibaldina di Sicilia e di Napoli nei Proclami, nelle Corrispondenze, nei Diarii del Tempo* (Turin, 1907).

On more specialized topics, taking first of all the early period in South America, there are, V. Varzea, *Garibaldi in America* (Rio de Janeiro, 1902), S. E. Pereda, *Garibaldi en el Uruguay* (3 vols., Montevideo, 1914), Anita Italia Garibaldi, *Garibaldi en América* (Buenos Aires, 1930), A. Villanueva, *Garibaldi en Entre Rios* (Buenos Aires, 1957), and S. Candido, *Giuseppe Garibaldi, Corsaro Riograndense* (Rome, 1964). For the years 1848–49, there is an excellent bibliography in Trevelyan; but above all there are the volumes by Loevinson and Hoffstetter already mentioned, and G. Spada, *Storia della Rivoluzione di Roma* (3 vols., Florence, 1868–1870). Probably the best account of the war of 1859 is F. Carrano, *I Cacciatori delle Alpi commandati dal Generale Garibaldi* (Turin, 1860). For 1860, Trevelyan once again gives a good bibliography; and special note should be made of G. C. Abba, *The Diary of one of Garibaldi's Thousand* (trans. E. R. Vincent, London, 1962), the works of Bandi and Forbes from which excerpts have been given earlier, and also C. Agrati, *Da Palermo al Volturno* (Milan, 1937).

For the 1860s, two first-hand accounts are G. Bruzzesi, *Dal Volturno ad Aspromonte* (Milan, n.d.), and G. Adamoli, *Da San Martino a Mentana* (Milan, 1892); and especially there is the biography by Guerzoni. Other personal contributions were made by G. Gadda, *Ricordi e Impressioni* (Turin, 1899), and F. Crispi, *Carteggi Politici Inediti—Aspromonte, Mentana* (Rome, 1912). For these later years, Jessie White Mario was also very close to Garibaldi: apart from her supplement to Werner's edition of the memoirs, there is her *La Vita di Giuseppe Garibaldi* (Milan, 1882), and *Garibaldi e i suoi tempi* (Milan, 1884). Among more recent studies, there are G. E. Curàtulo, *Il dissidio tra Mazzini e Garibaldi* (Milan, 1928); P. Fortini, *Giuseppe Garibaldi marinaio mercantile* (Rome, 1950) ; A. Luzio, *Aspromonte e Mentana, documenti inediti* (Florence, 1935), A. Luzio, *Garibaldi, Cavour, Verdi* (Turin, 1924), and C. Spellanzon, *Garibaldi* (Florence, 1958).

A great deal has been written about Garibaldi as a general. Recent works include *Garibaldi Condottiero* (by General Gazzera and others, an official War Office publication, Rome, 1932), L. Cicconetti, *Roma o Morte, 1867* (Milan, 1934), and P. Pieri, *Storia militare del risorgimento* (Turin, 1962). A good study of his generalship is G. Cadolini, "Garibaldi e l'arte della guerra" (*Nuova Antologia*, Rome, May, 1902), and "I Cacciatori delle Alpi" (*Nuova Antologia*, July, 1907). On his last campaign, that of 1870, Garibaldi's own chief of staff wrote an exaggerated justification—General J. P. T. Bordone, *Garibaldi et l'armée des Vosges* (Paris, 1871)—to which there were a number of strongly exaggerated replies, notably G. Theyras, *Garibaldi en France: Dôle, Autun, Dijon* (Autun, 1888).

The best full-length biography of Garibaldi, apart from that by his friend Guerzoni, is G. Sacerdote, *La Vita di Giuseppe Garibaldi* (Milan, 1933).

Index